Makery sewing

MITCHELL
BEAZLEY

For Lyra and Florrie, my treasures.

Makery Sewing
by Kate Smith

An Hachette UK Company
www.hachette.co.uk

First published in Great Britain in 2014
by Mitchell Beazley, an imprint of
Octopus Publishing Group Ltd,
Endeavour House, 189 Shaftesbury Avenue,
London, WC2H 8JY
www.octopusbooks.co.uk

Distributed in the US byHachette Book Group
1290 Avenue of the Americas,
4th and 5th Floors, New York, NY 10020

Distributed in Canada by Canadian Manda Group
664 Annette St., Toronto, Ontario, Canada M6S 2C8

ISBN 978 1 84533 888 6

A CIP catalogue record for this book is available
from the British Library
Printed and bound in China
10 9 8 7 6 5 4 3 2 1

Created by Harris + Wilson

Managing editor: Judy Barratt
Design: A-Side Studio
Photography: Marc Wilson and Ania Wawrzkowicz
Styling: Aliki Kirmitsi, Caroline Harris, Kate Smith
and Jaine Bevan
Editorial assistant: Emma Wynne
Illustrations: Martha Gavin

The use of glue, hammers and other materials
and tools as recommended in this book should
be done with care and in accordance with the
manufacturers' instructions. Although all
reasonable care has been taken in the preparation
of this book, neither the author nor the publisher
can accept any liability for any consequences
arising from the use of the book, or the information
contained within.

AUTHOR'S NOTE: SEWING MACHINE SETTINGS

Tension
Stitch tension is the cause of many a headache
for sewers. The tension dial controls the speed at
which the top thread flows through your machine.
If it's too tight, your top line of stitching will be really
taut and puckered. If it's too loose, your top line
of stitching will be loopy. I rarely fiddle with the
tension dial, but occasionally it will get knocked or
need adjustment. If that happens to you, I would
advise moving it only a very small bit at a time, then
testing your stitches to see if they have improved.

Stitch length
Most of the projects in the book call for a medium
stitch length, which is a number 3 on my machine.
If your stitches are too short, you may end up with
puckered sewing; too long, and your finished item
mightn't be as neat. Experiment with your machine
on a fabric scrap until you're happy with the effect.

Makery Sewing

OVER 30 PROJECTS FOR THE HOME, TO WEAR AND TO GIVE

KATE SMITH

MITCHELL
BEAZLEY

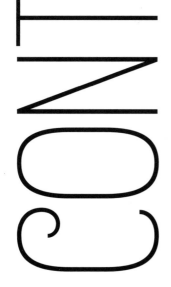

CONTENTS

INtRODUCtION

I've been sewing for as long as I can remember, inspired by my mum, gran and grandma, who always had projects on the go. It's in my blood.

One of my first 'real' projects was a sewing caddy for my mum, which I made out of some very 1980s floral Laura Ashley print. I remember so well the feeling of achievement I had. Seeing others experience that rush of accomplishment when we teach them to use a sewing machine is what motivates me now.

I have spent most of my life sewing for pleasure. I made my own clothes as a teenager, and I sewed to make some money throughout university. Once I started working, I spent an awful lot of my spare time making things, even though the first ten years of my career were in a totally unrelated (albeit creative) sector. Then, in 2009, I decided to change careers, and I opened The Makery, where we teach all sorts of creative skills to our customers.

I love the process of catching a glimpse of something that inspires me, or of dreaming up a unique idea, and then working with the fabric to make a pattern. Yet, these days, aside from making the odd dress for my daughters or curtains for our home, too much of my time is spent dealing with the admin of running The Makery. That's why writing this book has been such a joy. I've been able to spend time making my ideas come to life, and I've watched them unfold on the pages of the book – the excitement can be overwhelming!

Many of the visitors to our workshops come along with the intention of learning to sew, but are nervous about their ability, and often have an inherent fear of the sewing machine. To try to make friends with the machines at the workshops, our customers have named them all. We have Greta, Chardonnay, Dave, Susan, Dorothy – and

lots more. The real trick though, I think, is not to rush things. A sewing machine can be exasperating at times, so take your sewing journey steadily. Trying to tackle a complicated project too early on could knock your confidence. Start with the less tricky items in the book – something like the Patch Pocket Tee-shirt on page 40 or the Guest Towels on page 130. Work up to the Foldaway Bread Platter (page 116) or Pyjama Shorts (page 16) as you grow in confidence. If there is a sewing workshop near you, I encourage you to give it a try – it's nice to have someone to guide you through your first foray.

To make any of the projects, it's worth investing in a good pair of fabric scissors (keep them safe so no-one uses them for paper), glass-headed pins, needles, polyester thread in white, black and beige, and a smaller pair of embroidery scissors.

If you're a complete beginner, you may also need a sewing machine. There's no need to invest in one of the all-singing, all-dancing machines, but it is better to buy a reputable make that is nice and solid – the cheapest machines can end up being a false economy. Or ask around – you may find that a friend or relative has an unused machine tucked away and would be pleased to lend it to you. With regular servicing, some old machines can go on for years. They were built to last!

Whether you're new to this wonderful skill or a seasoned sewer, I really hope this book inspires you. Don't hesitate to ask if you have any questions – and please send us pictures of your projects! You can reach us at **facebook.com/themakery**, and check out our website at **www.themakery.co.uk**. Good luck with your sewing adventures!

Kate Smith
The Makery, Bath

smocked purse

TIME

ALLOW AN EVENING FOR THE SMOCKING AND ANOTHER EVENING TO ASSEMBLE THE PURSE, THEN A GOOD HOUR TO FIX THE CLASP. YOU'LL GET QUICKER WITH PRACTICE!

Who had a smocked dress when they were little? I did, and I adored it! Perhaps that's why I love this purse so much. I particularly like this style of smocking. It doesn't take too long, and looks so lovely with the simplest polka-dot fabric. Fixing the clasp takes patience, but the result shows off the smocking so well.

MATERIALS

OUTER POLKA-DOT FABRIC (1CM/¼IN POLKA DOTS, NOT LITTLE PIN DOTS): 56CM X 40CM (21¾IN X 16IN)

CO-ORDINATING POLYESTER THREAD

MEDIUM-WEIGHT IRON-ON INTERFACING: 42CM X 25CM (16½IN X 10IN)

LINING FABRIC: 42CM X 25CM (16½IN X 10IN)

SQUARE CLASP: 15.5CM (6⅛IN) AT ITS WIDEST POINT, BUT YOU CAN ADAPT THE PATTERN TO FIT ANY SIZE

PIPING CORD OR PAPER TWINE: 2 X 15CM (6IN) LENGTHS

CHAIN: 60CM (23½IN) LENGTH (OPTIONAL)

TOOLS

PATTERN PIECE PROVIDED AT THE BACK OF THE BOOK

TAPE MEASURE

FABRIC SCISSORS

NEEDLE

IRON

PINS

SEWING MACHINE

GLUE (WE RECOMMEND GÜTERMANN HT2 FABRIC GLUE OR UHU)

PLIERS (JEWELLERY PLIERS OR DIY TOOLBOX PLIERS WILL DO)

COCKTAIL STICK OR A PENCIL

SCRAP OF FABRIC OR FELT (TO PROTECT THE CLASP)

SMOCK THE OUTER FABRIC

1. Before you cut out the pattern pieces, you need to smock the fabric. You'll hand-sew four polka dots together to create a flower shape, as described below. You'll need to smock each short end of your spotty fabric.

2. Thread your needle and tie a knot at one end of the thread. Find the top left-hand diamond formation of dots in your fabric. Push your needle up through the back of the fabric, coming up at the base of the top dot in the diamond (see Figure 1). Continue stitching in and out of the polka dots as shown, finishing next to the point at which you started. Turn your fabric over and pull the thread tight. Secure with a knot.

3. Repeat Step 2, working your way down and across the fabric, as shown in Figure 2, so that you end up with smocking across the top of your fabric measuring 8cm (3¼in) deep.

4. Now repeat steps 2 and 3 on the other end of your outer fabric.

5. Trace and cut out the pattern piece. Fold the smocked fabric in half and place the pattern piece on top, as indicated on the pattern. Pin and cut out. You'll probably cut some of your smocked stitches, but don't worry.

MAKE THE PURSE POUCH

1. Iron the interfacing onto the wrong side of your lining fabric, following the manufacturer's instructions. Fold in half, place the pattern piece on top and cut out. Mark the two points A.

2. Fold the lining in half, right sides together. Pin in place and, with your machine set to straight stitch, sew down the two side seams, leaving a 1cm (¼in) seam allowance. Reverse stitch at the beginning and end to secure.

3. Now for the gusset. Put your hand inside the pouch and open out one of the bottom corners of the bag, so that the side seam is on top. Iron flat, so that the point forms a right angle. (See Figure 3, page 14.) Sew across the point, with a 2cm (¾in) seam allowance. Repeat for the other corner.

4. Now repeat steps 2 and 3 with the smocked outer fabric.

5. The following steps can get a bit fiddly. You should now have two pouches – one lining and one outer. Turn the outer pouch right side out, but keep the lining inside out. Sit the outer pouch inside the lining pouch, so that the right sides are facing. Match the side seams, and pin the outer to the lining around the top.

6. Place the pouch in front of you, so that one of the side seams is facing you. By hand (which is easier at this point), stitch from point A on one side of the seam to point A on the other side (your stitches will form a smile shape!). Sew through both fabrics, leaving a 1cm (¼in) seam allowance. (See Figure 4, page 14.)

7. Clip the curves, taking care not to cut your stitches. Turn the pouch around and repeat for the other side seam. Remove the pins.

8. Now scoop the outer fabric pouch out, and manoeuvre the lining pouch so that it sits inside the outer. You'll probably think you've made a mistake at this point and it will all seem a little bit wonky, but it will come right soon enough. Concentrate on one pouch at a time – outer, then lining. You should have a neatish, lined purse pouch when the pieces are correctly turned out.

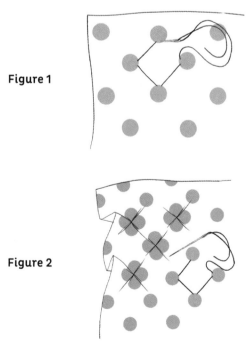

Figure 1

Figure 2

9. Match the top (raw) edges of fabric, lining to outer, on each side of the purse. Use running stitch (see page 148), close to the fabric edge, to hand-sew the pieces together, just to hold them in place while you attach the clasp.

ATTACH THE CLASP

1. OK, here we go … the nitty gritty. With the clasp fully open, drop some glue into the channel on one side. Not too thick – you don't want it to ooze out onto your fabric.

2. Take your pouch and match the centre point of one side of the pouch with the centre point of the glued side of the clasp (find the centre point by folding the pouch in half, matching the side seams). Make sure you have the clasp the right way round, so that its outside matches with the fabric outer of the purse.

3. Insert the fabric into the frame, nudging it in with a cocktail stick or pencil so that it is tucked right into the clasp channel (see Figure 5). When you're happy with the positioning, quickly push a length of the twine in between the fabric and clasp (on the interior side), to hold it in place and fill the gap between the fabric and clasp. You might find that when you push one side in, the other side comes out a bit. Stay with it!

4. With the first side of your purse fully inserted into the clasp, take your pliers and gently squeeze down on the clasp at either end. I like to pop a scrap of fabric or felt between the pliers and clasp so that the pliers don't leave scratches. Then gently squeeze down all the way around the frame to secure the fabric in place.

5. You'll notice that the twine extends beyond the end of the clasp – don't worry, just trim it off so that you can't see it.

6. Repeat these steps with the other side of the fabric pouch. You should find it slightly easier this time, as the fabric is already more or less held in place on the first side.

TIP

If you fancy attaching a chain as a shoulder strap, you could use a length of chain from a DIY store; or a necklace you pick up in a second-hand store.

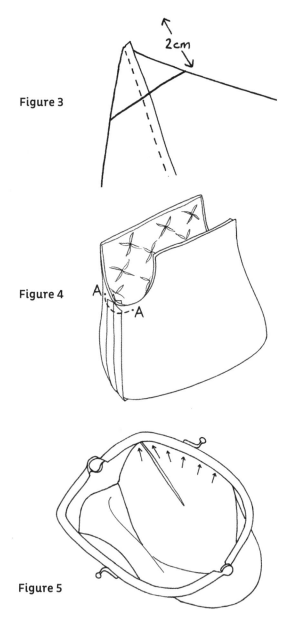

Figure 3

Figure 4

Figure 5

Pyjama Shorts

TIME

THIS IS QUITE A MEATY PROJECT – SET ASIDE A COUPLE OF EVENINGS OR EVEN A WEEKEND IF IT'S YOUR FIRST ATTEMPT.

What better reason to have a duvet day than these pyjama shorts? They are so gorgeous, I think you may just want to stay in them all day long! Once you know how to make them, I wouldn't be surprised if you worked up quite a collection of these, and they make the loveliest present.

MATERIALS

LIGHTWEIGHT COTTON FABRIC: 100CM X 110CM (40IN X 44IN)

CO-ORDINATING POLYESTER THREAD

TRIMMING: 150CM (60IN) (WE USED COTTON LACE)

RIBBON: 2CM (¾IN) WIDTH X 150CM (60IN) LENGTH

TOOLS

PATTERN PIECES PROVIDED AT THE BACK OF THE BOOK

TAPE MEASURE

PINS

FABRIC SCISSORS

TAILOR'S CHALK OR ERASABLE FABRIC PEN

SEWING MACHINE (WITH A BUTTONHOLE FOOT IF YOU HAVE ONE)

NEEDLE (IF YOU DON'T HAVE A BUTTONHOLE FOOT)

IRON

UNPICKER

SAFETY PIN

PREPARE YOUR FABRIC

1. Trace and cut out the pattern from the back of the book: you will need to cut the pattern in half as shown and widen or enlarge it in the middle section by the measurement written on the pattern, according to your size.

2. Fold your fabric in half widthways, right sides facing. Pin the template pieces onto your fabric and cut out around them through both layers. Mark the buttonhole lines on your fabric.

3. Set your sewing machine to zigzag stitch. Take one of your pieces of fabric and sew along the two curved edges. Keep your stitching close to the fabric edge – this will stop your fabric from fraying. Repeat for the other fabric piece.

STITCH THE LEG PIECES

1. Take your two pieces of fabric and lay them on top of each other, matching up the edges, right sides together. Pin in place.

2. With your machine set to straight stitch, sew through both layers of fabric along one of the curved edges, 1cm (¼in) in from the edge – just inside your zigzags (see Figure 1). Reverse at the start and end to secure. Open the seam and iron it flat. Repeat for the other curved edge.

3. Keeping the right sides of your fabric on the insides and the raw edges on the outside, fold the leg pieces so that the two seams you've just stitched are in the middle and lie on top of each other. Match short edge A with short edge B on one of your fabric pieces and pin together. Repeat for the other fabric piece. (Now of course the fabric is joined up; see Figure 2.)

4. Machine all the way along edges A and B on both sides, in one continuous line of sewing, 1cm (¼in) in from the fabric edge. Reverse stitch at the start and end to secure. (See Figure 2.)

MAKE THE WAISTBAND

1. Sew two buttonholes over the marks you made on the fabric. If you're hand-sewing the buttonholes, see page 152. Use an unpicker to open them up. If you're machine-stitching, refer to your manual.

2. With your shorts inside out, turn the waistband over by 1cm (¼in), then another 3cm (1⅛in) toward the wrong side. Pin and iron flat.

3. Machine stitch all the way round, 0.5cm (⅛in) above the bottom of the fold. This seam will create a channel for your ribbon. (See Figure 3.)

ADD THE FINISHING TOUCHES

1. First, the leg hems. Turn up the fabric for each leg by 1cm (¼in) and then 3cm (1⅛in), toward the wrong side. Pin and iron. Stitch around both hems, 0.5cm (⅛in) down from the top of the fold.

2. Position your trimming around one of the legs on the right side, over the stitching. Trim so that the ends of the lace meet. Pin in place and machine stitch to secure. Repeat for the other leg.

3. Finally, attach a safety pin to one end of your ribbon and thread it in through one buttonhole. Wiggle the pin through the waistband until it comes out of the other buttonhole.

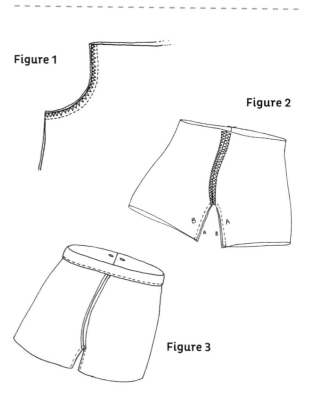

Figure 1

Figure 2

Figure 3

TIP

If you're using synthetic ribbon, singe the ends so they don't fray. Quickly wave the ribbon end over a flame, fusing the fibres together. (Be careful!) If you have natural ribbon, you can fold and stitch the ends to prevent them fraying.

CORSAGE HAIRBAND

TIME

THIS ISN'T TOO TAXING – YOU SHOULD BE ABLE TO MAKE IT IN AN AFTERNOON OR AN EVENING.

I first made one of these for my little girl to go to a party, but it quickly made its way into my collection, adorable as it is. It's really delicate – not too showy.

MATERIALS

WHITE OR CREAM TULLE (LIGHTWEIGHT NETTING FABRIC, SOMETIMES CALLED BRIDAL NETTING): ROUGHLY 120CM X 20CM (47¼IN X 8IN)

CO-ORDINATING POLYESTER THREAD

1 X VINTAGE BUTTON

NARROW RIBBON OR RIC-RAC: 0.5CM (⅛IN) WIDTH X 50CM (20IN) LENGTH

ELASTIC: 0.5CM (⅛IN) WIDTH X 10CM (4IN) LENGTH

TOOLS

PATTERN PIECE PROVIDED AT THE BACK OF THE BOOK

TAPE MEASURE

PENCIL

PAPER

PAPER SCISSORS

PINS

FABRIC SCISSORS

NEEDLE

CUT YOUR PETALS

1. Using your pencil and piece of paper, trace the petal pattern piece at the back of the book, and cut out with your paper scissors.

2. Fold the tulle fabric in half, then in half again (and even in half again if you like). Place the petal template on top of the fabric, toward the edge, pin in place and then cut around it using your fabric scissors. The fabric is so flimsy that you'll be able to cut out many petals at once to save time. And don't worry about being ridiculously neat with your cutting – this project is quite forgiving. Keep going, replacing and repinning the template, until you have cut out around 30 petal shapes. If you'd like a fuller flower, simply cut out more petals.

MAKE YOUR FLOWER

1. Thread your needle and tie a large knot at the loose end of the thread. Pinch one of the petals at the short straight edge. Make a couple of small stitches in the petal to hold the pinch in place.

2. Now pinch another petal and pass it right down the thread, so that it sits on top of the previous petal. Make a couple of stitches to hold the pinch in place. Continue with this method for all of your petals, placing them in a round shape as you go so that they form a flower (see Figure 1). You'll need at least two layers of petals – but you could add as many as you like.

3. When you've used up all the petals, secure the thread. Then, place the vintage button in the centre of the uppermost part of the flower to cover any untidy stitching; hand-sew in place and secure your thread with a good, tight knot.

PUT THE HAIRBAND TOGETHER

1. Hand-sew one end of the thin ribbon to one end of the elastic, making your stitching nice and secure. Place the ribbon and elastic around your head, so that it is slightly stretched. Cut to length, then stitch the other end of ribbon to the other end of the elastic.

2. Place the ribbon band around your head, and experiment with the position of the flower, holding it against your head and looking in a mirror. When you have decided, hold the flower in place on the ribbon as you take off the band and carefully hand-sew the back of the flower to the right side of the ribbon to hold it in place.

Figure 1

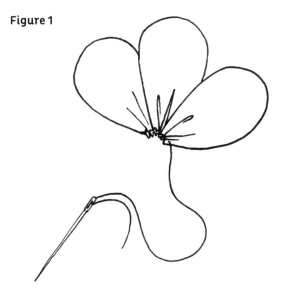

TIP

You could just as easily add the decoration to a hair slide or comb, or even to a pin to make a brooch. And you could scale it up, too, if you wanted something larger.

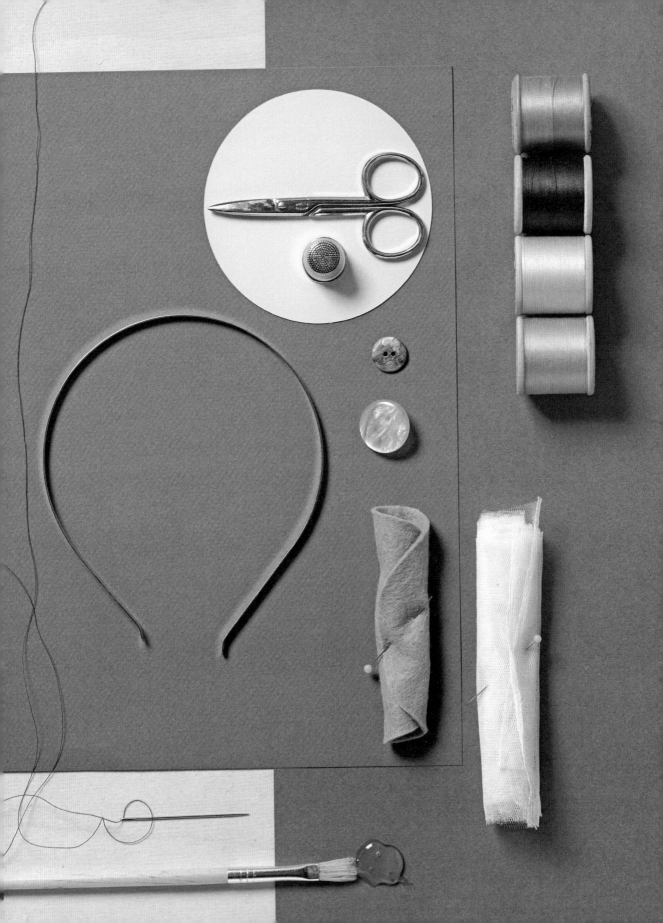

cosmetics bag

It's amazing – with a bow as a little added extra, this bag gains such elegance. I've used a neutral linen for the bag and a pretty, delicate cotton print for the bow, but most fabric types would work perfectly well. For example, you could try a luxuriously silky or velvet fabric to turn it into an extra-special evening bag.

MATERIALS

LARGE BOW FABRIC PIECE:
23CM X 23CM (9IN X 9IN)

SMALL BOW FABRIC PIECE:
8CM X 8CM (3¼IN X 3¼IN)

OUTER FABRIC: 22CM X 30CM
(8¾IN X 12IN)

LINING FABRIC: 22CM X 30CM
(8¾IN X 12IN)

CO-ORDINATING ZIP:
22CM (8¾IN)

CO-ORDINATING
POLYESTER THREAD

CONTRASTING POLYESTER
THREAD (OPTIONAL)

TOOLS

TAPE MEASURE

FABRIC SCISSORS

PINS

IRON

SEWING MACHINE
(WITH ZIPPER FOOT)

NEEDLE

TAILOR'S CHALK OR ERASABLE
FABRIC PEN

MAKE THE BOW

1. Fold the large bow fabric piece in half, right sides facing and matching the raw edges. Pin. With your machine set to straight stitch, sew along the unfolded raw edge of the fabric with a 1cm (¼in) seam allowance, to make a long, thin tube. Turn the tube the right way out and iron it so that the seam sits down the middle. Repeat this step for the small bow fabric piece.

2. Take the smaller tube (now ironed flat) and, seam downward, fold it in half so the short ends line up. Pin. Machine stitch along the short raw edges with a 1cm (¼in) seam allowance (see Figure 1), then trim the hem to 0.5cm (⅛in). Turn the tube right side out. Thread the larger bow piece through the tube, to form a bow shape (see Figure 2). You can slide the tube piece along to alter the look of the bow.

MAKE THE BAG

1. Place your bow on top of your outer fabric, right sides up. The side edges should more or less match. Position the bow so that it is 2cm (¾in) down from one of the short ends. Pin, then tack it down the sides, 0.5cm (⅛in) in from the edges.

2. To add the zip, take your lining fabric and fold each of the short ends under by 1cm (¼in) toward the wrong side. Iron the folds. Place one of the folded ends onto the underside of your zip, right side up. There should be a gap of around 4mm (⅙in) between the zip teeth and the fold. Pin. Attach a zipper foot to your machine and stitch this side of the zip, starting and finishing 3cm (1⅛in) in from each end of the fabric, reversing at the start and end. Repeat with the other short end of the lining and the other side of your zip. It's easier if you stitch with the zip open.

3. Turn each short end of outer fabric under by 1cm (¼in) toward the wrong side. Iron in place. Lay one of the ends onto the top side of the zip, so that the fold lies around 3mm (½in) from the zip teeth. You're making a zip sandwich – outer fabric on top, zip in the middle and lining underneath. Pin, then machine-stitch with your zipper foot to hold the fabric in place, starting and ending 3cm (1⅛in) in from each end of fabric.

Repeat for the other end of fabric on the other side of your zip – again, keep the zip open. (See Figure 3.)

4. Turn both outer and lining inside out, and open the zip about halfway. Place the lining pouch at the bottom and the outer pouch at the top – separated by the zip. Match up the side seams and pin in place. Pin the bulky edges by the zip seams down toward the lining fabric.

5. With the standard presser foot back on your machine, stitch down one of the side seams with a 1.5cm (½in) seam allowance – starting at the folded end of the outer, then sewing all the way down, over the zip, to the folded end of the lining. Be really careful to avoid the metal stopper when you sew over the zip teeth. I move the machine needle by hand, by bringing the balance wheel toward me, for this little section.

6. Repeat step 5 on the other side, but leave a gap of 7cm (2¾in) in the lining side, so that you have a hole to turn the bag right side out.

7. Turn the bag right side out through the gap in the lining, and use ladder stitch (see page 149) to hand-sew it closed. Sit the lining in the outer.

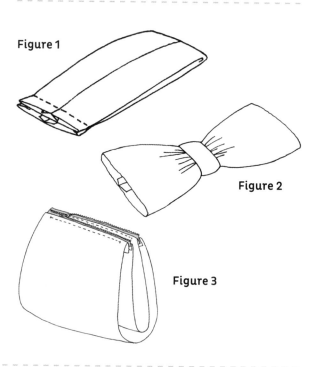

Figure 1

Figure 2

Figure 3

TIP

To make a swankier version of this for evening-wear, you could use a sumptuous velvet or sparkly fabric for the bow. Yes, please!

Pom Pom scarf

TIME

IF YOU HAVE A ZIPPER FOOT TO SEW THE POM POMS, THIS IS A PROJECT THAT YOU'LL GET DONE IN AN EVENING. ALLOW A BIT MORE TIME IF YOU'RE SEWING THE POM-POM TRIM BY HAND.

I love a good scarf. I'm often found wearing a sunny yellow one! And here's a revelation – you can make a scarf out of any fabric that takes your fancy. It could be a triangular wonder or a vast rectangular winter wrap-up. This neat little project produces a rather splendidly classy scarf with a pretty little pom-pom trim.

MATERIALS

LIGHT- TO MEDIUM-WEIGHT FABRIC: 100CM X 100CM (40IN X 40IN)

SMALL POM-POM TRIM: 200CM (80IN)

CO-ORDINATING POLYESTER THREAD

TOOLS

FABRIC SCISSORS

TAPE MEASURE

IRON

PINS

SEWING MACHINE (WITH ZIPPER FOOT)

NEEDLE

PREPARE THE SCARF

1. Cut your fabric into an isosceles triangle (remember those from Maths lessons?). Fold the fabric in half diagonally (see Figure 1) to cut a triangle that measures 100cm x 100cm x 140cm (40in x 40in x 55in).

2. This is a bit fiddly, but you don't want the edges to be too bulky so bear with it! Fold a double 0.5cm (⅛in) hem around all three edges, toward the wrong side of the fabric. Iron and pin in place as you go.

3. With your machine set to straight stitch, sew all the way around, keeping close to the inner folded edge. Reverse stitch at the beginning and end to secure.

ATTACH THE POM POMS

1. Take your pom-pom trim and pin it on the wrong side of the fabric on top of the hem, along the two shorter edges of your scarf. Position it so that the pom poms just poke out past the folded edge of the fabric, and the flat edge is flush with the hem. Pin in place, turning over and checking the positioning of your pom poms as you go. (See Figure 2.)

2. If you have a zipper foot, attach it to your machine and sew the pom-pom trim in place. If you don't have a zipper foot, you'll probably find it easier to stitch your trim in place by hand using running stitch (see page 148). Use stitches that are about 1cm (¼in) long, and keep the stitches in between the layers of fabric so that they don't show on the right side. Once you've attached the pom-pom trim, your scarf is done!

TIP

Don't cut the length of the pom-pom trim before you sew it, as you may just need a smidgen more.

Figure 1

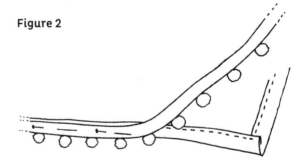

Figure 2

COLOURBLOCK CLUTCH

TIME

THIS IS A GOOD SUNDAY PROJECT – GIVE YOURSELF A BIT LONGER IF YOU'VE NEVER SEWN IN A ZIP BEFORE.

I love accessorizing, so I'm always looking for ways to reinvent the clutch bag. I thought I'd take the colourblock trend here and turn it into one of those great clutches that is really roomy!

MATERIALS

OUTER LIGHTWEIGHT COTTON FABRIC 1:
22CM X 62CM (8¾IN X 24½IN)

OUTER LIGHTWEIGHT CONTRASTING COTTON FABRIC 2:
22CM X 12CM (8¾IN X 4¾IN)

LINING FABRIC: 22CM X 60CM (8¾IN X 23½IN)

ZIP: 22CM (8¾IN)

1 X POPPER:
1CM (¼IN) DIAMETER

CO-ORDINATING POLYESTER THREAD

TOOLS

TAPE MEASURE

FABRIC SCISSORS

PINS

RULER

PENCIL

TAILOR'S CHALK OR ERASABLE FABRIC PEN

SEWING MACHINE (WITH ZIPPER FOOT)

IRON

NEEDLE

CUT YOUR OUTER FABRICS

1. Place outer fabric piece 1 in front of you, right side up. Take contrasting outer fabric piece 2 and place it on top, right side up again, matching the top and side edges. Pin in place.

2. Using your ruler and pencil, mark 5cm (2in) down from the top right edge. Then, mark 10cm (4in) down from the top left edge. Draw a line from the left- to the right-hand marks.

3. Cut through both layers of the fabric along the line (see Figure 1). Unpin the fabrics so that you have a bottom (larger) piece of outer fabric 1, and a top piece of contrasting outer fabric 2. These are the outer pieces from now on.

ADD THE ZIP

1. Place the two outer pieces on top of each other, right sides facing, lining up the cut diagonal edges. Pin. With your machine set to straight stitch, sew along the diagonal line with a 1cm (¼in) seam allowance. Reverse stitch at the beginning and end. Iron open the seam. (See Figure 2.)

2. To add the zip, fold each of the short ends of lining fabric under by 1cm (¼in) toward the wrong side. Iron the folds. Place one of the folded ends of fabric onto the underside of your zip, with the right side of the fabric facing up. There should be a gap of around 4mm (⅒in) between the zip teeth and the fold. Pin, then attach a zipper foot to your machine and stitch that side of the zip, starting and finishing 3cm (1⅛in) in from each end of the fabric, reversing at the start and end. Repeat with the other short end of the lining and the other side of your zip. It's easier to stitch with the zip open.

3. Turn each short end of the outer fabric under by 1cm (¼in) toward the wrong side. Iron in place. Lay one of the ends onto the top side of the zip, so that the fold lies around 3mm (½in) from the zip teeth. You're making a zip sandwich – outer fabric on top, zip in the middle and lining underneath. Pin in place, then machine stitch with your zipper foot to hold the fabric in place – starting and ending 3cm (1⅛in) in from each end. Repeat for the other end of fabric on the other side of your zip – it helps to keep the zip open. (See Figure 3, page 26.)

FINISH THE PURSE

1. Turn both outer and lining inside out and open the zip about halfway. Place the lining pouch at the bottom and the outer pouch at the top, separated by the zip. Match up the side seams and pin. Pin the bulky edges by the zip seams down toward the lining fabric. With the standard presser foot on your machine, stitch down one of the side seams with a 1cm (¼in) seam allowance. Start at the folded end of the outer, then sew all the way down – over the zip – to the folded end of the lining. Take care to avoid the stopper when you sew over the teeth. I like to move the machine needle by hand, turning the balance wheel toward me. Repeat for the other side, but leave a gap of 7cm (2¾in) in the lining.

2. Turn the bag right side out through the gap and use ladder stitch (see page 149) to hand-sew the last 7cm (2¾in) in the lining fabric closed.

3. Finally, fold the purse almost in half with the colourblock detail on the outside and bringing the short ends toward each other. You are going to attach the pieces of your snap fastener to the touching sides so that you can secure the purse in this position. Mark the points where you need to sew the fastener pieces. In turn, position each fastener piece and hand-sew in place, stitching through just one layer of fabric.

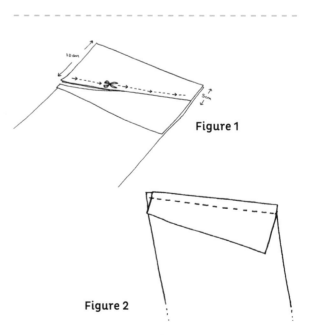

Figure 1

Figure 2

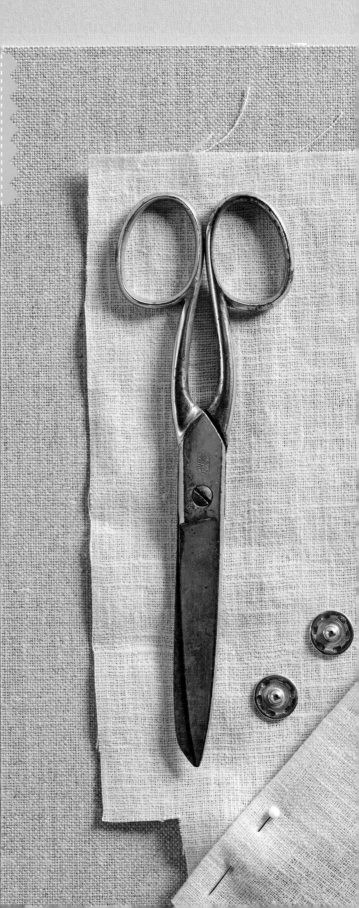

TIP

You can make this without the colourblock detail, if you prefer. Instead, have one outer piece of fabric measuring 22cm x 60cm (8¾in x 23½in), and begin at Add the Zip, step 2.

fabRic pendant

TIME

YOU'LL NEED JUST AN HOUR OR SO TO CREATE THIS GORGEOUS NECKLACE.

This project came about to solve a problem: I'm a fabric hoarder! I find it impossible to throw away those much-loved fabric remnants. They might be the last remains of a favourite print or pieces of generation-old clothing. Rather than stash them away in drawers, this project displays them for all to admire. I used a piece from a cross-stitch mat from a flea market.

MATERIALS

PENDANT FINDING

PIECE OF CARD (SUCH AS ONE SIDE OF A CEREAL BOX)

SMALL PIECE OF FABRIC OR EMBROIDERED CLOTH

CO-ORDINATING POLYESTER THREAD

PINCH OF POLYESTER STUFFING

TOOLS

PAPER SCISSORS

PENCIL

RULER

FABRIC SCISSORS

NEEDLE

GLUE (WE RECOMMEND GÜTERMANN HT2 OR A GLUE GUN)

CUT THE PENDANT FABRIC

1. Push the pendant finding face down onto the card, to make an indent of the pendant aperture shape. Cut out the shape from the card, shaving off an extra 1mm (1/16in) all the way around. This gives you a cardboard template.

2. Place the template onto your fabric, bearing in mind which section of the fabric you'd like to appear on the pendant. You could use the larger piece of card that you cut the template from as a window to view your fabric through and decide on your design. When you're happy with the positioning, draw a line 1.5cm (1/2in) larger than the edge of the template, all the way around. Cut out the fabric along your pencil line.

CONSTRUCT THE PENDANT

1. Thread your needle, and tie a large knot in the end of the thread. Sew a running stitch 0.5cm (1/8in) in from the edge of your fabric piece, all the way around. Keep your stitches nice and small – this will ensure you get a neater finish. Leave a longish loose thread when you have finished.

2. Take your pinch of polyester stuffing and pop it into your fabric on the wrong side.

3. Place the cardboard template onto the back of the stitched fabric, in the centre, to encase the stuffing. Pull on the loose end of your thread so that it gathers the fabric together around the cardboard. Pull tight, but make sure the cardboard piece doesn't bow. (See Figure 1.) Tie a knot to secure. Test the fabric for size by pressing it into the pendant finding. It may need a little coaxing, but it should go in and be nice and snug. Pop it out again for now so that you can attach it properly.

4. Put a generous blob of glue onto the front of the pendant finding. Push your fabric shape in place, pressing down firmly and holding it there for a few moments while the glue sticks. Leave it to dry according to the manufacturer's instructions – when it's dry you'll have a special pendant that showcases your beautiful fabric!

TIP

This could equally be a ring or brooch – you'd just need to purchase the appropriate setting. And you could always embroider some fabric yourself, or just use a piece of printed fabric instead.

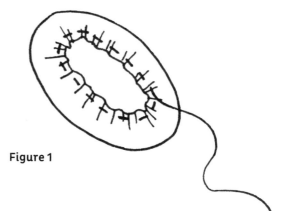

Figure 1

Patch Pocket tee-Shirt

I have a few random tee-shirts in my drawer that have remained unworn for a little too long. I also happen to have countless scraps of favourite fabric waiting to be shown off. Well, this project is the perfect marriage of the two. Best of all, it is very easy, very effective and oh-so totally unique.

MATERIALS

COTTON TOP OR TEE-SHIRT

SCRAP OF FABRIC – BIG ENOUGH TO FIT THE POCKET TEMPLATE

CO-ORDINATING OR CONTRASTING POLYESTER THREAD (YOUR CHOICE)

TOOLS

TEMPLATE PROVIDED AT THE BACK OF THE BOOK

PEN OR PENCIL

PAPER SCISSORS

PINS

TAILOR'S CHALK OR ERASABLE FABRIC PEN

FABRIC SCISSORS

IRON

SEWING MACHINE

CUT OUT YOUR PATCH

1. Trace and, using your paper scissors, cut out the pocket template at the back of the book. Don't forget to trace the arrows, too.

2. Take your patch fabric and place the pocket template on top, making sure the arrow on the pattern lines up with direction of the threads (the fabric grain). Pin to secure it in place, then using your tailor's chalk or erasable fabric pen, draw around the template. Cut the patch from the fabric along the line you have drawn.

SEW YOUR PATCH

1. Take your fabric patch and, along the top edge, fold over 1cm (¼in) toward the wrong side. Iron in place, then fold over another 2cm (¾in) in the same direction and iron again.

2. With your sewing machine set to straight stitch, sew along the bottom edge of this 2cm (¾in) seam. (See Figure 1.)

3. Fold over the remaining four edges by 1cm (¼in) toward the wrong side, and iron in place again, taking care at the corners to create a neat finish.

ATTACH YOUR PATCH POCKET

1. Iron your top or tee-shirt to remove any wrinkles, then lay it flat out in front of you, front upward. Pin the pocket in place. (See tip, above right.) Take care to pin the patch only to the top side of your tee-shirt.

2. Still with your machine set to straight stitch, starting at the top right corner of the pocket, sew all the way around the side and bottom pocket sides, stitching just 2mm (¹⁄₁₆in) in from your folded edges. (See Figure 2.) Each time you reach a corner, make sure the needle is down in the fabric, lift the presser foot up and pivot your pocket to line up the next length of stitching. Remember to place the presser foot down again before you continue stitching in the new direction. Don't forget that you're stitching only four of the sides, not the all-important fifth side – the pocket opening!

TIP

Once you've pinned your pocket on to your top, it's a good idea to try on the top (careful you don't prick yourself) and check before sewing that the pocket is in the correct position, and straight.

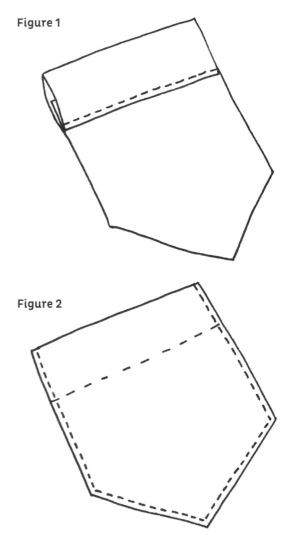

Figure 1

Figure 2

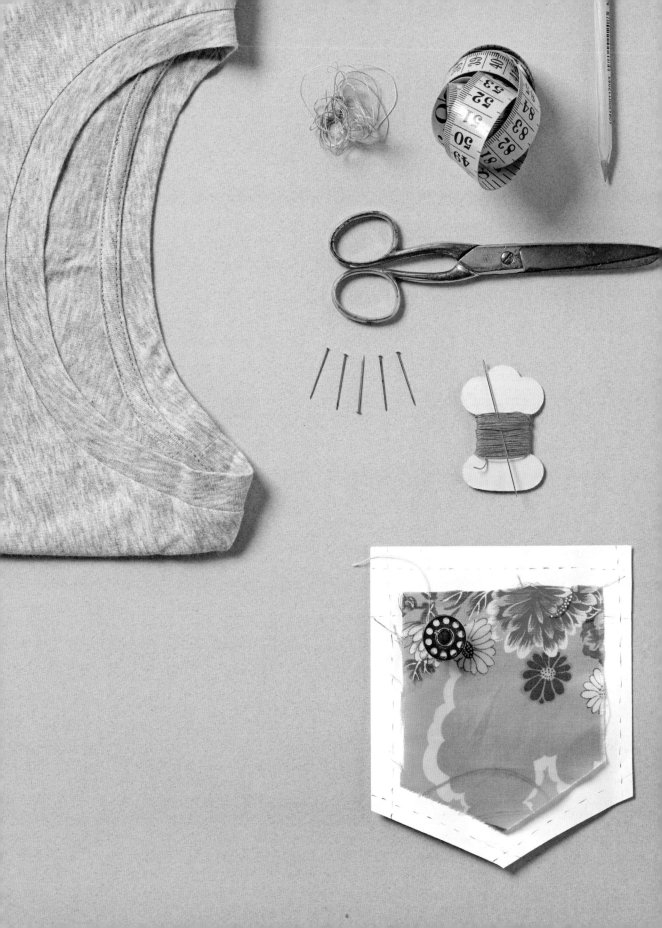

vintage belt bag

TIME

TAKE YOUR TIME WITH THIS PROJECT – ENJOY IT OVER A WEEKEND TO DO IT JUSTICE.

I adore vintage embroidered linen; the stories and hours of careful handiwork are so charming. And the colours are always so pretty. This is one of my favourite projects in the book – the delicate embroidery and worn leather look great together. I can't wait to use mine!

MATERIALS

LINEN OR MEDIUM- TO HEAVYWEIGHT COTTON FABRIC: 50CM X 70CM (20IN X 27½IN)

EMBROIDERED LINEN (SUCH AS A TABLE MAT, A CHAIR COVER OR PART OF A TABLECLOTH): APPROXIMATELY 30CM X 46CM (12IN X 18IN)

LINEN THREAD OR BUTTONHOLE THREAD

LEATHER BELT

CO-ORDINATING POLYESTER THREAD

TOOLS

TAPE MEASURE

FABRIC SCISSORS

IRON

PINS

SEWING MACHINE

TAILOR'S CHALK OR ERASABLE FABRIC PEN

PAPER SCISSORS

LEATHER HOLE PUNCH, OR BRADAWL AND HAMMER

NEEDLE

ATTACH THE FABRIC PIECES

1. If you have had to cut the embroidered cloth to the right size, fold all four edges under by 1cm (¼in) and iron them in place.

2. Position the embroidered cloth centrally on your fabric, right sides upward for both pieces, and pin in place. With your machine set to straight stitch, sew along the four sides of the embroidered cloth, roughly 0.5cm (⅛in) in from the edge to attach the fabric pieces together.

CREATE THE BAG

1. We're going to make French seams to keep it nice and neat. Fold the fabric in half so the short ends line up, wrong sides facing (your embroidered piece should be on the outside), matching up the sides and ends. Pin the sides together, then machine stitch each side seam with a 0.5cm (⅛in) seam allowance (see Figure 1).

2. Turn the bag inside out and iron flat, pushing the side seams out completely. Machine stitch the two side seams again, but this time with a 1cm (¼in) seam allowance – so that you contain the first seam and raw edges within.

3. Now to create a gusset in the bottom of the bag. Turn the bag right side out. Take one of the side seams and fold it in toward the bottom of the bag, until the corner makes a triangle. Pin flat. Measure 4cm (1½in) down your seam from the corner point and draw a line across, perpendicular to your seam, with tailor's chalk or the fabric pen (see Figure 2). Machine stitch along this line. Reverse stitch at the start and end to secure. Repeat for the other corner.

4. To neaten the top of the bag, fold over the top edge by 1cm (¼in), then 3cm (1⅛in) toward the inside, all the way round the bag. Pin in place. Machine stitch 2cm (¾in) down from the edge. Reverse stitch at the start and end to secure.

ATTACH THE HANDLES

1. Cut the buckle off your belt with some sharp scissors (but not your fabric scissors). Cut the remaining belt in half to make two strips of equal length. Take your hole punch or bradawl and hammer, and make eight holes in each end of both strips of leather (see Figure 3).

2. On both sides of the bag, measure 16cm (6¼in) in from each side seam along the top (opening) edge. Use pins to mark each of these four points – these are where you'll attach the handles. Place one end of one of the handles in position, and hand-sew in place using your extra-strong thread, making an X shape for each set of four holes (see photograph, page 44). Go over the stitching two or three times to make sure it's nice and strong. Secure on the inside with a knot. Repeat the process to attach the remaining three ends of the handles.

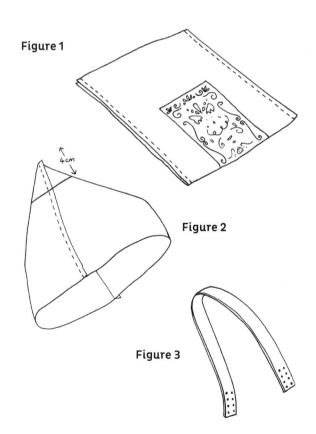

Figure 1

Figure 2

Figure 3

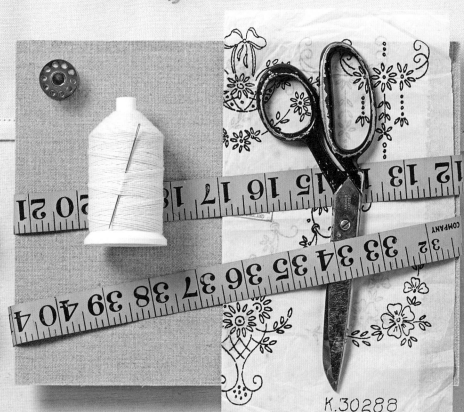

K.30288

TIP

If you don't have any old leather belts or embroidered linen to hand, have a look in your local second-hand stores – they can be a treasure-trove of crafting gems. Vintage clothes shops usually have a supply of cheap leather belts, too.

skinny bow belt

TIME

THIS PROJECT BENEFITS FROM PRECISION – TAKE YOUR TIME OVER THE MEASURING, PINNING, IRONING AND TOPSTITCHING. ALLOW AROUND THREE HOURS ALTOGETHER.

What better way to upscale an outfit than with a gorgeous, bespoke belt. From floral patterns to gingham or tweed, you can choose your fabric to suit the occasion. We've gone all out here and used neon and gold. The bow is detachable, so you can wear the belt with or without it, or you could make lots of interchangeable bows.

MATERIALS

BELT FABRIC: 8CM X 110CM (3¼IN X 44IN)

MEDIUM-WEIGHT IRON-ON INTERFACING: 8CM X 110CM (3¼IN X 44IN)

BOW FABRIC: 13CM X 11CM (5¼IN X 4¼IN)

LOOP FABRIC: 7CM X 5CM (2¾IN X 2IN)

TALL SLIDE BUCKLE (SOMETIMES CALLED A 'SLIDE'): 2CM (¾IN)

CO-ORDINATING OR CONTRASTING POLYESTER THREAD (YOUR CHOICE)

TOOLS

TAPE MEASURE

FABRIC SCISSORS

IRON

PINS

SEWING MACHINE

SEW THE BELT

1. Place the interfacing on the wrong side of the belt fabric and iron on, following the manufacturer's instructions.

2. Fold the short ends over by 1cm (¼in) toward the wrong side and iron in place.

3. Now fold the fabric in half lengthways with the wrong sides facing, and iron flat. Open the fabric out, then fold each of the long edges in toward the central fold, so they meet in the middle. Pin and iron in place.

4. Remove the pins and fold the fabric in half lengthways again. Pin to secure. With your machine set to straight stitch, sew all the way around all four edges, 3mm (⅛in) in from the edge, catching in all the layers.

MAKE YOUR BOW

1. Fold the bow fabric in half lengthways, right sides together and matching the raw edges, to make a tube. Machine stitch along the long edge, with a 1cm (¼in) seam allowance, leaving a gap in the middle of about 4cm (1½in).

2. Open out the seam and re-position it so that it falls in the middle of the bow piece. Pin and stitch along both short ends. (See Figure 1.)

3. Turn the bow right side out through the gap. (There's no need to iron, as you're looking for a bit of flounce in the bow.)

PUT THE BELT TOGETHER

1. Take the fabric for the loop and fold it in half, right sides together, so the long raw edges meet, to make a long tube. Machine stitch along the long edge, with a 0.5cm (⅛in) seam allowance. Turn it right side out so that the seam is in the centre, as for the bow, and then iron flat.

2. Fold in half, with the seam on the outside of the tube, and stitch along the short edge with a 0.5cm (⅛in) seam allowance. Turn it the right way out.

3. Feed the bow piece through the loop to form your bow. Now thread the belt through the back of the loop behind the bow.

4. Thread the belt through the slide buckle, and back through by 3cm (1⅛in). Stitch to secure, reversing to hold firmly in place (see Figure 2).

TIP

If you'd like a wider belt, you just need to find a wider slide buckle and then adjust the fabric measurements accordingly: measure the inside width of the buckle, then multiply it by four for the new fabric width measurement. The bow loop dimension will also need adjusting: multiply the inner slide buckle measurement by two, and add 3cm (1⅛in). All other directions and dimensions remain the same.

Figure 1

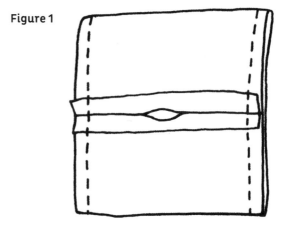

Figure 2

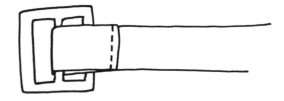

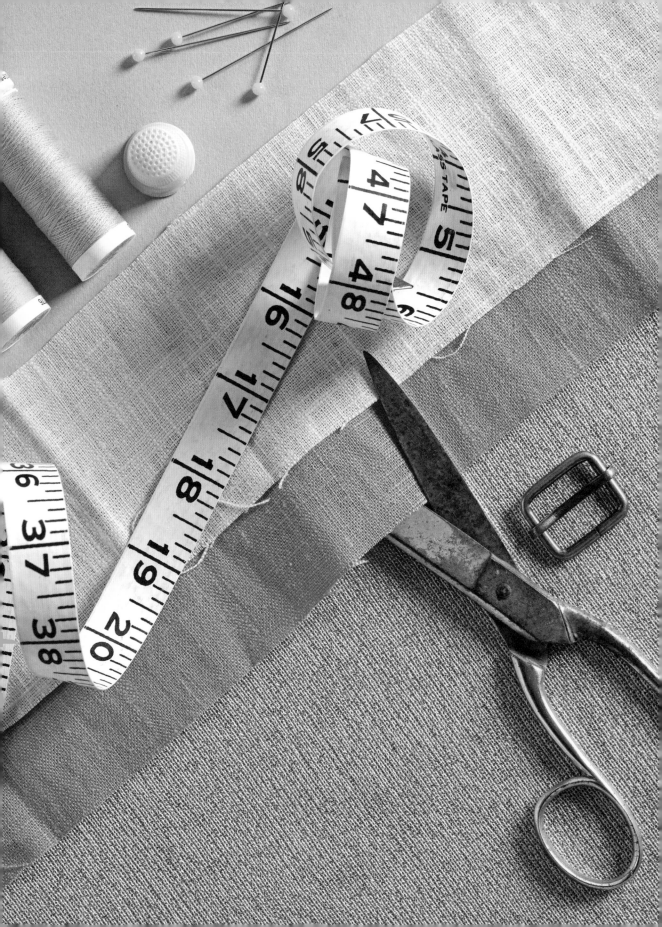

Dog Collar

TIME

GIVE TWO OR THREE HOURS TO MAKING THIS SPECIAL TREAT FOR YOUR FAVOURITE POOCH.

Rufus, our beloved Makery spaniel, looks like a superstar in this collar, but please don't tell him – it'll go straight to his head! Rufus is a small to medium-sized dog, but you can easily alter the measurements if you want to make the collar bigger for a more substantial pooch – just take a look at the tip box on page 54 for instructions how.

MATERIALS

MEDIUM-WEIGHT IRON-ON INTERFACING: 62CM X 9CM (24½IN X 3¾IN)

STRONG COTTON FABRIC (IT'S IMPORTANT THAT THIS ISN'T TOO FLIMSY): 62CM X 9CM (24½IN X 3¾IN)

CO-ORDINATING OR CONTRASTING POLYESTER THREAD (YOUR CHOICE)

SIDE-RELEASE BUCKLE: 2.5CM (1IN) WIDTH

D-RING: 2.5CM (1IN) WIDTH

COTTON SIDE RIBBON: 2CM (¾IN) WIDTH X 4CM (1½IN) LENGTH

TOOLS

TAPE MEASURE

TAILOR'S CHALK OR ERASABLE FABRIC PEN

FABRIC SCISSORS

IRON

PINS

SEWING MACHINE

PREPARE YOUR FABRIC STRIP

1. Following the manufacturer's instructions, iron the interfacing onto the wrong side of your fabric piece.

2. Fold the fabric in half to create a long thin strip, wrong sides together. Iron the fold in place.

3. Unfold your fabric. Take one of the short ends, and fold it over by 1cm (¼in) toward the wrong side. Iron in place. Repeat for the other short end.

4. Using the long central fold line as a marker, fold the two long edges inward so that they meet at the fold line. Iron in place. (See Figure 1.)

5. Finally fold up along your initial central, long fold line, tucking all the folded edges inside. Iron again just to make sure it's nice and crisp, then pin it in place along the long edge.

SEW THE COLLAR

1. With your machine set to straight stitch, sew along one short edge, turn to sew along the long edge that you've pinned together and then turn again to sew along the final short edge. Try to stay 0.5cm (⅛in) in from the fabric edge. Reverse stitch at the start and end to secure.

ATTACH THE COLLAR FASTENING

1. Take your side-release buckle and thread one end of the fabric through the gap on the 'holder' part of the buckle. (Rather than the 'clasp' part.) Pull the fabric through by 3cm (1⅛in), then fold it back on itself. Pin together and machine-stitch through all the layers of fabric to hold the buckle in place (see Figure 2). It's really important these stitches are very secure, so make sure you reverse over your stitching several times to reinforce it and ensure the stitches don't come loose.

2. Now for the D-ring – this will hold the loose end of fabric in place once the collar is on your pet and is a good for attaching your pet's name tag. Take your length of ribbon and turn each short end over by 0.5cm (⅛in) toward the wrong side, and iron to hold it in place. Work out where you'd like the D-ring to go, then take your ribbon and place it on the right side of your fabric collar, at the D-ring position. Pin in place with

Figure 1

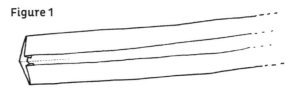

Figure 2

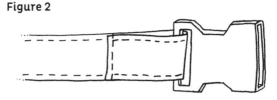

Figure 3

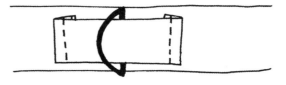

the D-ring looped on. Machine-stitch each end of the ribbon, making sure you reverse several times to ensure it's strong. (See Figure 3.)

3. Now thread the loose end of the collar through the gap in the other part of the buckle (the 'clasp' part). Fold it back on itself, then pop it through the D-ring to hold it in place.

eye mask

TIME

SET ASIDE AN AFTERNOON OR A COUPLE OF EVENINGS TO COMPLETE THIS PROJECT.

In their crusade for practicality, some items leave style at the door, but not this gorgeous eye mask. You need only a small amount of fabric for this project – I used some beautifully soft tana lawn for extra comfort over weary eyes. This is a great gift for someone leaving on their travels, or who frequently flies long-distance.

MATERIALS

FRONT AND LINING LIGHTWEIGHT COTTON FABRIC: 2 X PIECES EACH MEASURING 14CM X 23CM (5½IN X 9IN)

HEADBAND LIGHTWEIGHT COTTON FABRIC: 5CM X 60CM (2IN X 23½IN)

BINDING LIGHTWEIGHT COTTON FABRIC: 50CM X 50CM (20IN X 20IN); OR 70CM (27½IN) BIAS BINDING (2.5CM/1IN WIDTH)

CO-ORDINATING POLYESTER THREAD

ELASTIC: 0.5CM (⅛IN) WIDTH X 40CM (16IN) LENGTH

COTTON INTERLINING OR BATTING, OR WOOL FELT: 14CM X 23CM (5½IN X 9IN) UP TO 0.5CM (⅛IN) THICK

TOOLS

PATTERN PIECE PROVIDED AT THE BACK OF THE BOOK

TAPE MEASURE

FABRIC SCISSORS

TAILOR'S CHALK OR ERASABLE FABRIC PEN (OPTIONAL)

PINS

IRON

SEWING MACHINE

2 X SAFETY PINS

NEEDLE

PREPARE YOUR FABRIC

1. Using the eye-mask pattern, cut out two pieces of fabric and one piece of interlining or batting. Mark the band points on the lining fabric with pins or tailor's chalk, as indicated on the pattern piece.

2. Lay the three fabric pieces on top of each other so the edges all line up. Start with the lining, placing it right side down, then layer on the interlining/batting, and top with the front fabric, placed right side up. Pin the three layers together. With your machine set to straight stitch, sew round the outside edge – about 2mm (⅛in) in from the edge. The stitching will hold the layers together for the next steps.

MAKE THE HEADBAND

1. Take the long, thin piece of headband fabric and fold over 1cm (¼in) along each of the long edges, toward the wrong side. Pin and iron in place. Fold the fabric strip in half lengthways, wrong sides together, and iron and pin to secure. Machine stitch all the way along the long open side of the rectangle, sewing 2mm (⅛in) in from the edge. Ensure you stitch through all the layers of fabric. You should now have a long thin tube.

2. Attach a safety pin to each end of the elastic. Thread one safety pin through the fabric tube. The fabric will ruche as you thread the elastic through (the other safety pin will stop the fabric coming off the end of the elastic).

3. Machine stitch the elastic in place at each end of the ruched tube, to stop it slipping. Ensure the fabric and elastic aren't twisted (see Figure 1).

4. Remove the safety pins. Trim the ends of elastic so that they're flush with the fabric. Pin each end of the headband in place on the lining side of the mask, making sure you line up the raw edges. Now do a couple of machine stitches to hold in place (see Figure 2).

ATTACH THE BINDING

1. Read pages 150–51 for directions on how to make your own bias binding, using your 50cm (20in) square of fabric. You need to make 70cm (27½in) of bias binding.

2. Fold one of the short ends of the bias binding over by 1cm (¼in) toward the inside to create a neat end. Iron in place. Open out the bias binding and place it on top of the eye mask as shown (the right side of the bias should face the right side of the eye mask). Pin it all the way around, easing it around the corners for a neat finish. Machine stitch in place, in the fold of the bias binding (see Figure 3).

3. Flip the bias over the raw edges of the eye mask, toward the back. Use ladder stitch (see page 149) to hand-sew the bias binding in place (see Figure 3) to conceal all the raw edges.

> **TIP**
>
> You can pad the mask with either a wool felt or cotton interlining or batting, but whatever you use, opt for a natural fabric rather than synthetic so that it doesn't sweat!

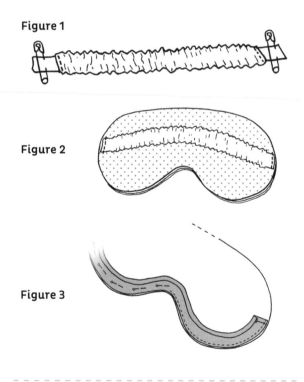

Figure 1

Figure 2

Figure 3

60

BOOK COVER

TIME

PUT ASIDE A COUPLE OF EVENINGS FOR THIS PROJECT. I SUGGEST ONE EVENING TO MEASURE AND CUT OUT THE FABRIC PIECES AND ONE FOR THE SEWING. THE COVER CAN BE A BIT OF A FIDDLE, SO TAKE YOUR TIME.

A diary, travel journal or wedding scrapbook is so special and personal that making a unique cover for it seems just the right thing to do. You could adapt the measurements to cover your most precious books, if you prefer – whatever takes your fancy.

TOOLS

RULER

TAILOR'S CHALK OR ERASABLE FABRIC PEN

TAPE MEASURE

FABRIC SCISSORS

PINS

SEWING MACHINE

IRON

NEEDLE

MATERIALS

OUTER LIGHTWEIGHT COTTON FABRIC: 35CM X 60CM (13¾IN X 23½IN)

COTTON OR POLYESTER LIGHTWEIGHT BATTING OR WADDING: 50CM X 35CM (20IN X 13¾IN)

INNER LIGHTWEIGHT COTTON FABRIC: 100CM X 35CM (40IN X 13¾IN)

CO-ORDINATING POLYESTER THREAD

ELASTIC (FOR A PEN OR PENCIL LOOP): 1CM (¼IN) WIDTH X 6CM (2⅓IN) LENGTH

CONTRASTING POLYESTER THREAD (OPTIONAL)

1 X POPPER: 1CM (¼IN) DIAMETER

CUT OUT YOUR PIECES

1. Begin with cutting the outer and batting fabric. Place the outer fabric wrong side up on a flat surface. Take the book you are going to cover and open it out flat on the fabric. Using the ruler and tailor's chalk or erasable fabric pen, measure and mark a line 3.5cm (1⅓in) wider than each side of the book. The distance between these two lines is width X. Then, measure and mark a line 2cm (¾in) above and below the top and bottom of the book. The distance between these two lines is height Y. Join the lines to form a rectangle and cut out. (See Figure 1.)

2. Cut a piece of batting to the same size as the outer fabric.

3. Now for the two pockets that will hold the book in place, on the inner fabric mark out two rectangles measuring height Y x 10cm (4in). Cut out the rectangles.

4. For the lining, on the remaining inner fabric, mark out a rectangle measuring height Y x width X minus 10cm (4in). Cut out. (See Figure 1.)

5. Finally, the clasp. From the remaining outer fabric, cut two rectangles measuring 10cm (4in) x 5cm (2in). (See Figure 1.)

SEW THE POCKETS AND CLASP

1. Take one of the pocket pieces and turn a 1cm (¼in) hem toward the wrong side on the height Y right-hand edge. Pin in place. Take the other pocket and turn a 1cm (¼in) hem on the height Y left-hand edge. Pin in place. With your sewing machine set to straight stitch, sew along both hems, 0.5cm (⅛in) in from the edge.

2. Lay the two rectangles for the clasp on top of each other, right sides facing. Machine stitch along one long edge, continue in a curve along the top and then go down the other long edge, leaving a 1cm (¼in) seam allowance. The stitching will form a long U-shape, and leave one of the short ends open. Clip the curves (see Figure 2, page 66).

3. Turn the clasp right side out and iron flat, then topstitch around the seamed edges, leaving a 2mm (¹⁄₁₆in) margin.

Figure 1

TIP

To help you get perfectly
curved corners, draw around
a cotton reel.

PUT THE COVER TOGETHER

1. The order in which you lay out the pieces is important – it will all come out the right way when you've stitched the cover together, so bear with it. On a flat surface, lay down first the batting, then the outer fabric right side up.

2. Place the clasp at the centre of the left-hand (height Y) edge, facing inward so that the raw edges are lined up. Fold the piece of elastic in half and place it on top of the centre of the clasp piece, raw edges matching up. Pin in place. (See Figure 3.) Machine stitch the clasp 0.5cm (⅛in) in from the edge to hold in place.

3. Take the two pockets and place them on top, one at each side of the cover, right sides facing down and seamed edges toward the centre.

4. Take the lining piece. Place it right side facing down, centred on top of the pile of fabrics, so there is a 5cm (2in) gap at each side edge. The top and bottom edges should line up. Pin everything safely in place to keep the layers together (see Figure 4).

5. Sew all the way around the cover, 1cm (¼in) in from the edge, curving your stitching at the corners (see Figure 5). Clip the corners (see page 150).

ADD THE FINISHING TOUCHES

1. Now the exciting part: turn the cover the right way out through one of the gaps in the lining. Make sure you push right into the corners. Iron the cover flat.

2. Topstitch 2mm (⅛in) in from the edge all around the outside of the book cover – you can use a matching or contrasting thread for this, whichever you prefer. (See Figure 6.)

3. Put your book inside its cover and mark where the clasp should come when the book is closed. Mark where the popper needs to sit, and hand-sew it in place through one layer of fabric.

Figure 4

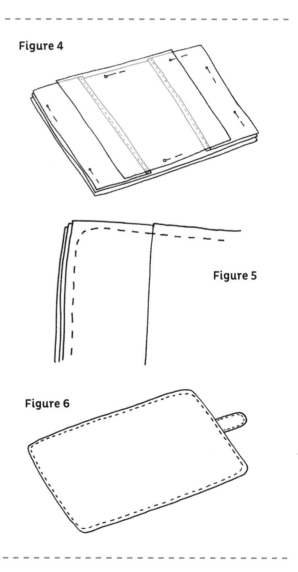

Figure 5

Figure 2

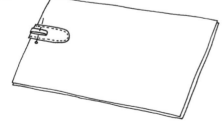

Figure 3

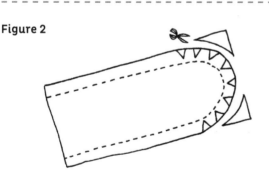

Figure 6

Hooped laundry bag

Ugh, laundry! There's far too much of it in my house. This excellent bag does, however, manage to brighten up the process a little. It even makes the act of tidying the laundry quite fun of an evening – who can throw their dirty socks through the hoop and straight into the bag?

TIME

A COUPLE OF EVENINGS AT YOUR MACHINE SHOULD DO IT!

TOOLS

TAPE MEASURE

TAILOR'S CHALK OR ERASABLE FABRIC PEN

FABRIC SCISSORS

PINS

SEWING MACHINE

IRON

SAFETY PIN

MATERIALS

OUTER LIGHTWEIGHT COTTON FABRIC:
40CM X 110CM (16IN X 44IN)

LINING LIGHTWEIGHT COTTON FABRIC:
40CM X 110CM (16IN X 44IN)

PIPING CORD: 150CM (60IN)

CO-ORDINATING POLYESTER THREAD

EMBROIDERY HOOP:
23CM (9IN) DIAMETER

MAKE THE BAG

1. Fold your outer fabric in half widthways, right sides together – you'll have a rectangle measuring 40cm x 55cm (16in x 21½in). Pin down the two long sides (making sure you leave the top edge open). Repeat for the lining fabric.

2. With your sewing machine set to straight stitch, sew down the long sides of the outer fabric with a 1cm (¼in) seam allowance. Iron the seams open, making sure they sit nice and flat. This is your outer bag. Repeat for the lining.

3. Turn the outer bag right side out, and insert it into the lining bag so that the right sides of both bags are touching and the side seams match up.

4. Pin the lining to the outer around the top open edge. Machine stitch around the top of the bag 1cm (¼in) down from the edge, and leaving a 10cm (4in) gap to turn the bag through. Reverse stitch at the beginning and end to secure.

5. Turn the whole bag the right way out, through the 10cm (4in) gap. Flatten out the bag, and iron the top seam so that the crease is nice and crisp.

INSERT THE DRAWSTRING AND HOOP

1. Turn the top edge over toward the outside by 7cm (2¾in), like a cuff, so that the lining fabric shows on the outside of the bag. Pin in place. Starting 17cm (6¾in) from one of the side seams, machine stitch along the lower edge of the cuff, leaving a 0.5cm (⅛in) seam allowance and finishing your stitching 4cm (1½in) before you get back to the start to leave gap (see Figure 1). Reverse stitch at the start and end to secure.

2. Attach a safety pin to the end of the piping cord and thread it through the gap, feeding it all the way through the channel and out again. Even up the exposed lengths of piping cord and knot the ends together. You now have a drawstring bag.

3. To fit the top of your bag into the embroidery hoop, pop the smaller hoop inside the top edge of the bag, just under the piping cord. Loosen the larger hoop and pop it on the outside of the bag, at the same point as the smaller hoop. Tighten it in place. Hang up your bag and let the sock-throwing games commence!

Figure 1

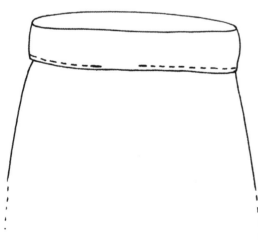

TIP

You don't need to include the embroidery hoop if you'd rather not – you could stop at the last step 2 and have a drawstring laundry bag instead. Come to think of it, you can use the drawstring bag for any purpose you like.

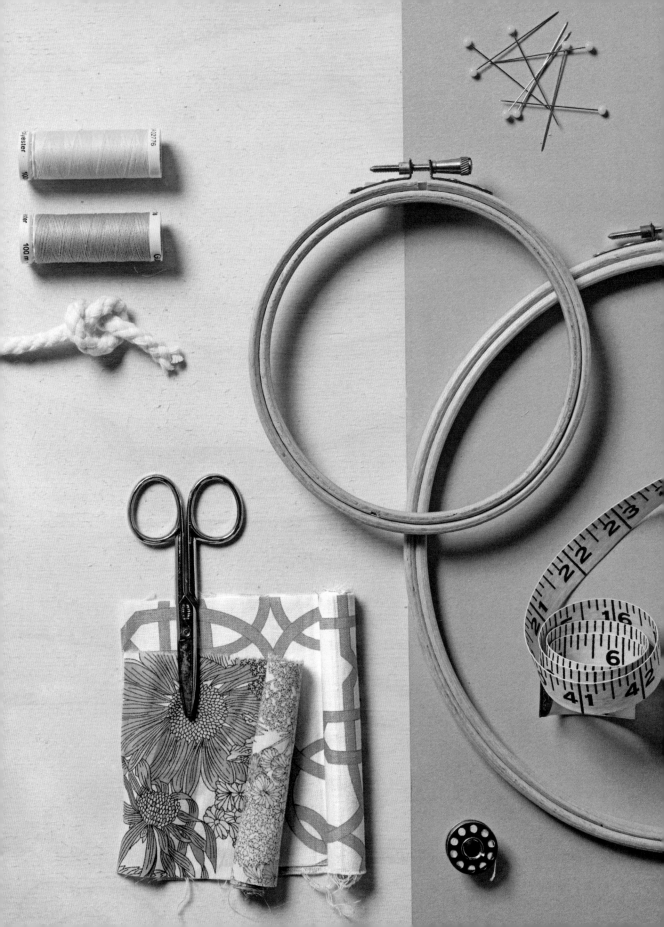

LiPStiCK-hOldeR KeyRiNg

TIME

ALLOW A COUPLE OF HOURS TO AN EVENING FOR THIS SIMPLE PROJECT.

No more rummaging about in your bag for the lipstick you know is in there somewhere – with this neat lipstick-holder keyring, you just need to find your keys! In fact, you can use this to house anything – lipstick, lip balm, USB stick – whatever you like. Simply adapt the measurements to suit.

MATERIALS

LIGHTWEIGHT COTTON TRIM FABRIC: 6.5CM X 14CM (2½IN X 5½IN)

PATTERNED LIGHTWEIGHT COTTON FABRIC: 6.5CM X 22CM (2½IN X 8¾IN)

CO-ORDINATING POLYESTER THREAD

1 X PIECE WIDER RIBBON: UP TO 1CM (¼IN) WIDTH X 4CM (1½IN) LENGTH

2 X PIECES NARROW RIBBON: 3MM (½IN) WIDTH X 20CM (8IN) LENGTH

SPLIT-RING KEYRING

VELCRO OR POPPER FASTENER (OPTIONAL, SEE TIP ON PAGE 74)

TOOLS

TAPE MEASURE

FABRIC SCISSORS

SEWING MACHINE

IRON

PINS

ATTACH THE PIECES

1. Place the trim fabric on top of the patterned fabric, right sides together, matching the short edges at one end. With your machine set to straight stitch, sew the short edges together, with a 1cm (¼in) seam allowance, to make one long piece. Iron flat.

2. Turn under one of the short ends by 1cm (¼in) toward the wrong side and machine stitch in place with a 0.5cm (⅛in) seam allowance. Repeat for the other short end.

3. Lay the fabric in front of you, right side up, with the trim fabric at the top. Fold the 4cm (1½in) length of ribbon in half, wrong sides together, and place it 17cm (6¾in) up from the hem at the bottom of the fabric, on the right side. Pin to secure. (See Figure 1.)

4. Using one of the narrow pieces of ribbon, put one end, right side down, where the trim meets the patterned fabric, matching the raw edges. Coil up the ribbon and pin so it won't get in the way when you stitch the seams. Repeat on the other side with the other piece of ribbon. (See Figure 1.)

SEW THE HOLDER TOGETHER

1. With the right side of the fabric still uppermost, fold up the bottom of the fabric by 7cm (2¾in). Pin in place and then fold the top down by 9cm (3¾in), so that it overlaps. (See Figure 2.)

2. Stitch down the two sides, all the way from top to bottom, with a 1cm (¼in) seam allowance, taking care to catch in all the layers (including the ribbon). Reverse stitch at the beginning and end to secure.

3. Clip the corners (see page 150) and turn the holder right side out, making sure that you push out all the way into the corners.

4. Slide the split-ring keyring on to the ribbon loop. Once your lipstick is in place, fold over the flap of fabric and wrap around, then tie the ribbon to hold it in place.

> ### TIP
> If you are making a holder for a man – perhaps to house a USB stick – omit the ribbon and instead stitch on a square of Velcro or a popper to fasten the holder together.

Figure 1

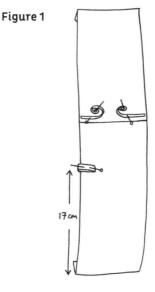

17cm

Figure 2

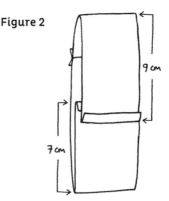

9 cm

7 cm

Handmade tie

TIME

THIS WILL TAKE AN EVENING OR TWO, DEPENDING ON HOW CONFIDENT YOU ARE WITH SEWING BY HAND, AS MUCH OF THE CONSTRUCTION IS DONE IN THIS WAY.

Ties can be really expensive, and the choice of fabrics is often limited. My gorgeous friend Lucy made this tie for my husband when he was best man at her wedding. With the remnants she made the magnets from our first Makery book, and has put up wedding pictures on her fridge with them. Such a lovely idea!

TOOLS

PAPER

PENCIL

TAPE MEASURE

PAPER SCISSORS

IRON

FABRIC SCISSORS

PINS

SEWING MACHINE

NEEDLE

MATERIALS

PATTERN PIECES PROVIDED AT THE BACK OF THE BOOK

TIE UPPER LIGHTWEIGHT COTTON FABRIC, SUCH AS TANA LAWN: 75CM X 75CM (30IN X 30IN)

LINING LIGHTWEIGHT COTTON FABRIC: 25CM X 30CM (10IN X 12IN)

LIGHTWEIGHT IRON-ON INTERFACING: 75CM X 75CM (30IN X 30IN)

CO-ORDINATING POLYESTER THREAD

PREPARE THE UPPER AND LINING PIECES

1. Trace all the tie pattern pieces at the back of the book and cut them out using your paper scissors.

2. Lay the upper fabric out in front of you and iron it flat. Place the upper pattern pieces, 1, 2 and 3, on the bias (see page 152). Pin in place. Using your fabric scissors, cut out the three pieces.

3. Iron the interfacing on to the back of the tie upper pieces, following the manufacturer's instructions.

4. Join piece 1 to 2 and 2 to 3, right sides together. Pin in place, matching the notches. With your machine set to straight stitch, sew together with a 1cm (¼in) seam allowance. (See Figure 1.) Trim the ends of the seams that poke out at each side, so they are flush with the edges. Open out and press the seams flat.

5. Iron the lining fabric flat, then lay the lining pattern pieces on the lining fabric, on the bias. Cut out.

NEATEN THE POINTS AND SEW UP THE TIE

1. Fold up the points of each lining piece by 1cm (¼in) toward the wrong side (see Figure 2). Now fold in the two sides by 1cm (¼in). (See Figure 3.) Pin in place and iron flat. This is called a mitred corner – just so you know!

2. Repeat these folds on the two ends of the upper fabric, and pin and iron as before. At both ends, use ladder stitch (see page 149) to hand-sew the two edges of the hem together where they meet at the point, so that your point is crisp.

3. Lay out the upper fabric, wrong side up. Position the larger lining triangle, right side up, on the point of the larger end of the tie, leaving a margin of 2mm (¹⁄₁₆in) from the end. Ladder stitch the lining in place along the bottom-edge V shape.

4. Repeat with the smaller triangle at the smaller end of the tie.

5. Turn both long edges of the tie in by 1cm (¼in), toward the wrong side. Iron in place. (See Figure 4.) Fold both of those edges in toward the middle of the tie so that they meet in the middle. Hand-sew the two sides together using ladder stitch, all the way down the length of the tie.

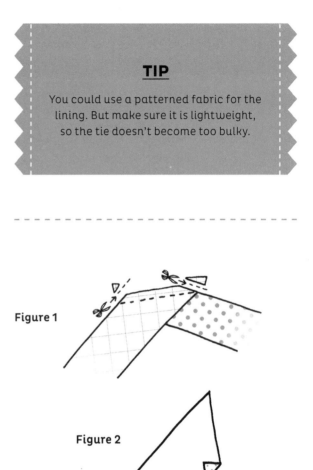

Figure 1

Figure 2

Figure 3

Figure 4

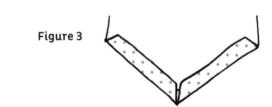

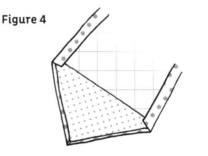

picnic cutlery wraps

TIME

ALLOW A COUPLE OF HOURS TO AN EVENING FOR THIS STRAIGHTFORWARD PROJECT.

Who doesn't love a picnic? Packing everything up specially is part of the fun. If you're not going on a picnic, these can liven up lunchtime any day, wherever you are. Open out the wraps, take out the cutlery and put the wraps on your lap to double as napkins.

MATERIALS

FOR TWO WRAPS:
2 X CONTRASTING LIGHTWEIGHT COTTON OR LINEN FABRIC SQUARES, CUT ALONG THE FABRIC GRAIN: 50CM (20IN) X 50CM (20IN) EACH

CO-ORDINATING POLYESTER THREAD

CO-ORDINATING OR CONTRASTING RIBBON OR TAPE (UP TO 1CM/¼IN WIDTH), OR TWINE: 2 X 60CM (23½IN) LENGTHS

TOOLS

TAPE MEASURE

RULER

TAILOR'S CHALK OR ERASABLE FABRIC PEN

FABRIC SCISSORS

PINS

SEWING MACHINE

IRON

SEW YOUR PICNIC WRAPS

1. Take each square of fabric and measure and mark a line 13cm (5¼in) up from the bottom edge. Cut off this 13cm (5¼in) x 50cm (20in) strip, keeping it nice and neat – it will form the cutlery pocket.

2. On one of the 13cm (5¼in) pocket strips, fold a double 1cm (¼in) hem along the top edge, toward the wrong side. Pin in place. With your sewing machine set to straight stitch, sew the hem with a 0.5cm (⅛in) seam allowance. Repeat for the other strip.

3. Pair the fabric pieces, mixing and matching so that you have a contrasting pocket. Place the pocket strip on top of the large rectangle, with the right sides of both fabrics facing upward and matching the bottom and side raw edges. Pin in place.

4. Turn the fabric over so that it is wrong side up. Create a double hem by folding over 0.5cm (⅛in) fabric and then another 1cm (¼in) along each of the four edges. Pin in place and iron, then machine stitch, close to the inner fold, making sure you catch in all the layers of fabric. Repeat steps 3 and 4 for the second wrap.

5. Measure the pocket piece into three equal-sized parts (they should be roughly 15.5cm/6⅛in each) to hold your cutlery. Use your chalk or fabric pen to draw two lines on the pocket to mark the thirds. Machine stitch a neat line along the two drawn lines (see Figure 1). Reverse stitch at the beginning and end to secure. Repeat for the second wrap.

ADD THE TIES

1. If you are using ribbon or tape, neaten each end: turn under a 0.5cm (⅛in) hem and stitch in place. If you are using twine, tie a small knot near the end of the twine to stop it fraying.

2. Find the centre of the ribbon, tape or twine and position it about 1cm (¼in) down from the top of the pocket on the right-hand hem. Machine stitch in place with five or six stitches, in line with the hem, reversing a couple of times to hold the tie firmly in place. (See Figure 2.)

Figure 2

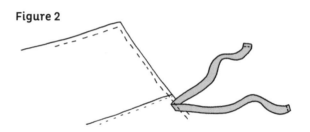

Figure 1

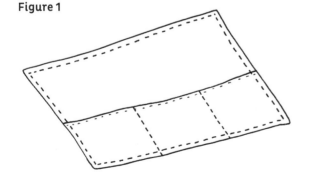

TIP

This makes such a lovely gift – you could make a set for a family or a special occasion, and even embellish each with an initial, if you like.

shower hat

You might think a shower hat belongs in the 1950s, but don't knock it till you've tried it! Once you have one at the ready, you won't look back. Everyone I've made this for has loved it. Make sure to choose pretty fabric – small prints work best.

MATERIALS

OUTER LIGHTWEIGHT COTTON FABRIC:
50CM X 50CM (20IN X 20IN)

WATERPROOF LINING FABRIC (SEE TIP, PAGE 86):
50CM X 50CM (20IN X 20IN)

CO-ORDINATING POLYESTER THREAD

ELASTIC: 1CM (¼IN) WIDTH (MAXIMUM) X 60CM (23½IN) LENGTH

TOOLS

STRING OR THREAD

PENCIL

TAPE MEASURE

ERASABLE FABRIC PEN

FABRIC SCISSORS

PINS

SEWING MACHINE

2 X SAFETY PINS

CUT AND SEW YOUR SHOWER HAT

1. You're going to make a homemade set of compasses so that you can draw a perfect circle on your fabric. Tie one end of a piece of string or thread around a pencil. Measure out 24cm (9½in) of string and tie the fabric pen onto the string at this point. Place the tip of the pencil at the centre of your lining fabric (you can find this easily by folding the fabric into quarters). Hold the pencil tip in place, then pull the string taut, and use the fabric pen to draw a circle on the fabric, keeping the pencil in the centre. The circle should be 48cm (18¾in) in diameter.

2. Cut out this fabric circle, then use it as a template to cut out a circle the same size from the outer fabric. (Alternatively, you could cut out a paper template and use it to cut both fabric circles.)

3. Put the two fabric circles together, right sides facing. Pin in place. With your machine set to straight stitch, sew around the outside edge of the circles with a 0.5cm (⅛in) seam allowance, leaving a gap of 8cm (3¼in) in your stitching.

THREAD THE ELASTIC

1. Turn the shower hat right side out through the gap, making sure you push the circle flat right up to the seam. Spread the shower hat fabric completely flat and pin (see Figure 1).

2. Make a line of stitching on the right side of the fabric, 2cm (¾in) in from the edge, all the way around the circle.

3. Attach a safety pin to each end of your elastic. Pin one end to the fabric, to anchor the elastic. Feed the other safety pin through the gap in the stitching and around the perimeter of the shower hat, through your casing. It should become beautifully ruched. When you get back to the beginning, knot the ends of elastic together and remove the safety pins.

4. Try the hat on for size, and tighten or loosen the knot so that the cap fits just right. When you're happy, tie the elastic with a double or treble knot to secure and snip the ends leaving only about 0.5cm (⅛in) free. Wiggle the knot around in the casing so that it isn't in line with the gap.

5. Fold in the edges of the outer and lining fabric at the gap. Pin in place and machine stitch closed, as close to the edge as you can – about 2–3mm (⅛in) in if possible!

Figure 1

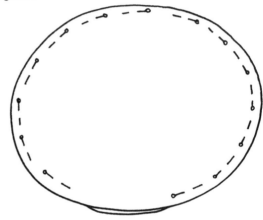

TIPS

I've tried making this shower hat with many different fabrics, and the best waterproof fabric I've found for it is a cheap fabric shower curtain! It flows through the machine with ease, whereas other waterproof fabrics tend to stick and make life tricky. If you can't find a cheap shower curtain, the best way I've found to sew with PVC fabric is to stick some masking tape to the underside of your presser foot to help the fabric glide through.

Pincushion

TIME

IT'S THE EMBROIDERY THAT TAKES THE TIME HERE – ALLOW A COUPLE OF EVENINGS FOR THAT. THE CONSTRUCTION, THOUGH, IS MUCH QUICKER – JUST AN HOUR OR SO.

The inspiration for this project comes from all the beautiful Japanese fabrics we stock in the shop, and traditional Japanese sashiko embroidery. I've tried to create a similar effect with a simple pattern of running stitch. A pincushion is a really great gift for anyone crafty.

MATERIALS

TOP PLAIN LINEN OR COTTON FABRIC SQUARE: 20CM (8IN) X 20CM (8IN)

BACKING PLAIN LINEN OR COTTON FABRIC SQUARE: 10CM (4IN) X 10CM (4IN)

EMBROIDERY THREADS IN FOUR COLOURS OF YOUR CHOICE

CO-ORDINATING POLYESTER THREAD

POLYESTER FILLING: 15G (½OZ)

TOOLS

EMBROIDERY DESIGNS PROVIDED AT THE BACK OF THE BOOK (THE PHOTOGRAPH SHOWS DESIGN 1)

FOR THE TRANSFER, ONE OF THE FOLLOWING:
• IF YOUR TOP FABRIC IS QUITE SEE-THROUGH: MASKING TAPE AND AN ERASABLE FABRIC PEN OR PENCIL
OR
• FOR THICKER TOP FABRIC: WATER-SOLUBLE FABRIC STABILIZER (SEE PAGE 154); PENCIL AND BOWL

NEEDLE

FABRIC SCISSORS

EMBROIDERY HOOP: 15CM (6IN) DIAMETER

IRON

PINS

SEWING MACHINE

EMBROIDER YOUR PINCUSHION

1. **For thinner top fabric:** Iron the top fabric flat. Centre it on top of your chosen embroidery design (1 or 2), right side up, and hold it in place with masking tape. Trace the pattern onto the fabric using the fabric pen. Proceed to step 2.

   For thicker top fabric: Centre the water-soluble fabric stabilizer on top of your chosen embroidery design (1 or 2), and trace the pattern onto it using a pencil. Cut around your design, then peel off the back and stick it down onto the centre of your top fabric. You will embroider through both layers. Proceed to Step 2.

2. Pop your fabric into the embroidery hoop, making sure it's stretched nice and flat.

3. Pick a colour of embroidery thread and choose one line on the template to stitch. Hand-sew along the lines with running stitch (see page 148). Repeat with the other three colours and lines.

4. **For thinner fabric:** Iron the embroidered fabric flat on the wrong side.

   For thicker fabric: Submerge the fabric under warm water and leave it for a couple of minutes, gently agitating it to help the soluble layer disappear. Leave to dry, then iron flat.

PUT THE PINCUSHION TOGETHER

1. Lay the two squares of fabric right sides facing, centring the backing fabric over the embroidered design. With your machine set to straight stitch, sew around the four sides of the backing fabric with a 1cm (¼in) seam allowance. Leave a 4cm (1½in) gap in the middle of one of the sides for the stuffing. Trim the front fabric to the same size as the backing fabric (see Figure 1). Clip the corners (see page 150).

2. Turn the cushion right side out, making sure you push fully into the corners, and stuff it with the polyester filling. Push in plenty of stuffing to make it quite firm.

3. Turn in the two raw edges of the gap and hand-sew together with ladder stitch (see page 149).

TIP

Don't feel limited to using the pattern I chose for the pincushion (the one shown in the photograph on page 88). I've given another option (pattern template 2) in the back of the book, too. Or, you can freestyle!

Figure 1

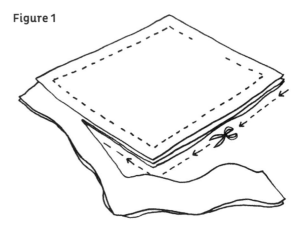

Tool apron

This project started life as a gardening apron – a handy place to keep garden tools while you're digging, planting and pruning. Then I realized that actually it could serve as an apron for any purpose. Whether you need it to keep your spoons and whisks at the ready in the kitchen or for your tape measure, scissors and threads in your craft studio, this tool apron will do the job. You can choose the size of the pockets to fit your tools – simply sew the pocket seams at appropriate intervals. Hey presto! You have a functional, but classy little number.

MATERIALS

HEAVYWEIGHT COTTON OR LINEN FABRIC: 50CM (20IN) X 60CM (23½IN)

BIAS BINDING: 2.5CM (1IN) WIDTH X 200CM (79IN) LENGTH

CO-ORDINATING POLYESTER THREAD

COTTON RIBBON OR TAPE: 4CM (1½IN) WIDTH X 150CM (60IN) LENGTH

TOOLS

TAPE MEASURE

FABRIC SCISSORS

PINS

SEWING MACHINE

IRON

TAILOR'S CHALK OR ERASABLE FABRIC PEN

PREPARE YOUR FABRIC

1. First, you're going to attach the bias binding to the bottom (60cm/23½in) edge of the fabric. Cut a length of bias binding to 60cm (23¾in). Open it up and place it on top of the fabric with right sides facing and lining up the raw edges. Pin the bias binding in place. (See pages 150–51 for how to make your own bias binding.)

2. Machine stitch in place along the fold line of the bias binding. Reverse stitch at the beginning and end to secure your stitches. (See Figure 1.) Trim back the raw edge of this seam to 0.5cm (⅛in) – this will make the next step easier.

3. Fold over the 1cm (¼in) of extra bias at each short end, wrong sides together. Now fold the long edge of the bias over the raw edges and your stitching line, to the other side. Pin in place so that the folded edge of the bias lies beyond the line of stitching. On the right side of the fabric, sew down the ditch ensuring that you catch the bias on the back in the line of stitching. (See Figure 2.)

MAKE THE POCKETS

1. Lay the piece of fabric you've been working with out in front of you (wrong side facing up) and fold up the bottom by 18cm (7in) to create the pocket band. Pin and iron in place.

2. Now decide how many pockets you'd like and how big you'd like them to be. When you have decided, mark the vertical lines on the folded fabric using your tailor's chalk or your fabric pen and stitch a straight line from the bottom (the folded edge) up to the top (where the bias is). Reverse stitch at the beginning and end of each line to secure your stitching.

FINISH THE SIDES

1. To add the bias down the sides of the apron, repeat steps 1, 2 and 3 of Prepare Your Fabric (above) for each side edge. This time, add 1cm (¼in) extra bias to the bottom and fold up and create a neat edge (don't worry about neatening the top as this will get tucked into the waistband).

MAKE THE WAISTBAND

1. Fold your ribbon or tape in half to find the centre and mark the spot with a pin. Fold the ribbon or tape in half lengthways to create a long V-shaped channel to slot the apron into.

2. Find the centre of your apron fabric. Match this point to the centre of the ribbon or tape, slotting the apron fabric into the V. Pin in place.

FINISH THE APRON

1. To create a finishing touch, take the remaining bias binding and turn the short edges under so that it is the same width as your apron, then tuck this up into the apron band so that half of it is poking out (see Figure 3), unpinning the waistband and re-pinning as you go.

2. Sew all the way along the ribbon or tape, keeping your stitching about 0.5cm (⅛in) up from the bottom of the tape. Reverse stitch at the beginning and end to secure.

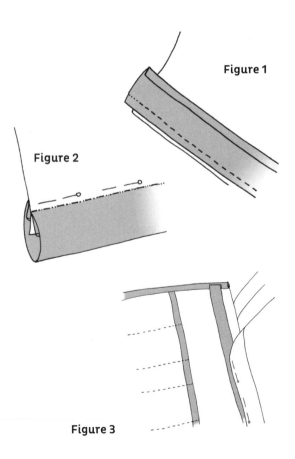

Figure 1

Figure 2

Figure 3

Men's washbag

TIME

THIS IS ONE OF THE BOOK'S MOST COMPLICATED PROJECTS, SO PERHAPS DON'T ATTEMPT IT UNTIL YOU'RE CONFIDENT WITH USING A SEWING MACHINE. IT MAY TAKE A FULL WEEKEND TO COMPLETE.

Okay, so the title is men's washbag. But, of course, it could be for anyone. I just wanted to make a project that would be a great gift for a man, really. I've seen these lurking in our bathroom when friends come to visit, so thought I'd make a pattern for one. It will hold a lot of loot – nifty!

MATERIALS

LINING OILCLOTH OR COTTON/LINEN FABRIC: 30CM X 65CM (12IN X 26IN)

POCKET OILCLOTH OR COTTON/LINEN FABRIC: 3 X 30CM X 32CM (12IN X 12¾IN)

IRON-ON VINYL (IF NOT USING OILCLOTH): 30CM X 65CM (12IN X 26IN) AND 30CM X 96CM (12IN X 37¾IN)

3 X ZIPS IN A CONTRASTING OR CO-ORDINATING COLOUR: 30CM (12IN) EACH

OUTER HEAVYWEIGHT COTTON OR LINEN FABRIC: 30CM X 65CM (12IN X 26IN)

RIBBON (I USED COTTON RIBBON): 8CM (3¼IN) LENGTH

METAL RING FOR HANGING, SUCH AS A KEYRING LOOP

BIAS BINDING: 2.5CM (1IN) WIDTH X 200CM (79IN) LENGTH

1 X POPPER: 1CM (¼IN) DIAMETER

TOOLS

IRON

TAPE MEASURE

TAILOR'S CHALK OR ERASABLE FABRIC PEN

FABRIC SCISSORS

PINS

SEWING MACHINE (WITH ZIPPER FOOT)

NEEDLE

MASKING TAPE OR TISSUE PAPER (OPTIONAL; SEE TIP, PAGE 99)

PREPARE THE FABRIC AND SEW IN THE ZIPS

1. If you are not using oilcloth, iron the two vinyl pieces on to the right side of the fabric lining and the right side of the pocket fabric pieces, following the manufacturer's instructions.

2. Take one of the pocket pieces and cut a strip measuring 7cm x 30cm (2¾in x 12in) from the top. (Make sure it is the top of the fabric if the fabric you've chosen has a direction, such as the camera pattern I used.)

3. Place one of the zips along the top edge of the larger piece of pocket fabric, right sides together and lining up the raw edges. Pin in place. Attach the zipper foot to your machine and set it to straight stitch. Sew along the zip, above the teeth but keeping close to them. (See Figure 1.) Reverse stitch at beginning and end to secure. For details on how to put in a zip, see page 152.

4. Lay the other side of the zip face down onto the bottom edge of the smaller pocket piece, right sides together and lining up the raw edges. Sew as before, with a straight stitch along the zip, close to the teeth. (See Figure 2.)

5. Iron the layers of fabric away from the zip, both above and below the zip. Then, on the right side, topstitch a line 0.5cm (⅛in) away from each seam to hold the fabric in place and keep the zipper teeth free of any tangles. (See Figure 3.) Repeat steps 1–5 for the other two pockets, ensuring you place the zips in the same direction each time.

Figure 3

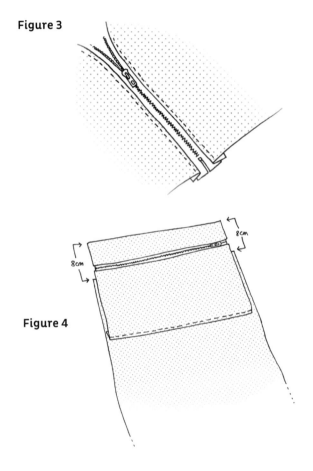

Figure 4

Figure 1

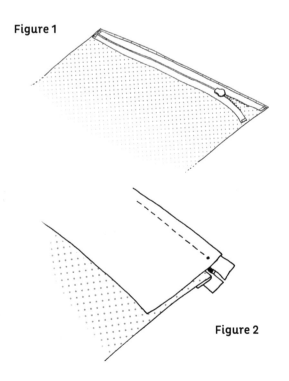

Figure 2

MAKE THE POCKETS

1. First you're going to attach the top pocket to the washbag. Take one of the pocket pieces and turn under the bottom edge by 1cm (¼in). Then, place it onto the lining (both the lining and pocket should be right sides facing up), so that the top of the pocket overhangs the top of the lining by 8cm (3¼in). Pin in place, then machine stitch along the bottom edge of the pocket to hold in place, with a 0.5cm (⅛in) seam allowance. (See Figure 4.)

TIPS

Some oilcloths can be tricky to sew, so rather than invest in an expensive Teflon-coated presser foot, place a layer of tissue or masking tape over the areas you want to sew. Stitch through it, then carefully tear off the paper or tape after you've stitched. Or instead of iron-on vinyl or oilcloth, you could use a waterproof fabric shower curtain.

2. Line up the top and side raw edges of this pocket with the lining. There should be excess pocket fabric at the bottom. Fold this into a concertina (see Figure 5), and pin in place. Machine stitch the folds close to the side raw edges – just to hold them secure while you work on the next steps.

3. To make the middle pocket, take another pocket piece and turn the top edge under by 1cm (¼in). Position it onto the lining, 4cm (1½in) below the top pocket. Line up the side edges. Pin in place, then machine stitch along the top edge of the pocket with a 0.5cm (⅛in) seam allowance. Measure 19cm (7¾in) down from the top of this pocket piece on the lining fabric, and pin the bottom of the pocket in place at that point, turning the bottom edge of the pocket under by 1cm (¼in) as you go. (See Figure 6.) Machine stitch with a 0.5cm (⅛in) seam allowance. Fold the excess fabric at the bottom of the pocket into a concertina as before, and stitch in place at the sides again.

4. To make the bottom pocket, take the final pocket piece. Turn the top edge under by 1cm (¼in). Position it onto the lining, 4cm (1½in) below the bottom of the middle pocket. Line up the side edges. Pin, then machine stitch along the top edge of the pocket with a 0.5cm (⅛in) seam allowance. Measure 18cm (7¼in) down from the top of this pocket piece, and pin the bottom of the pocket at that point – there should be 1cm (¼in) of lining fabric below this pocket piece, to which you will attach the bias binding. Machine stitch the pocket in place with a 0.5cm (⅛in) seam allowance. Fold the excess fabric at the bottom of the pocket into a concertina as before, and stitch in place at the sides again.

FINISH THE WASHBAG

1. Turn the washbag over and place the outer fabric on top, wrong sides facing and lining up the raw edges. Pin in place. Sew along both long sides, 2mm (¹⁄₁₆in) in from the edge, catching in all the layers (pockets and all).

2. Thread your length of ribbon through the ring, fold it in half and place it on the centre of the top of the washbag on the pocket side, lining up the raw edges. Pin in place. Sew along the top of the washbag, with a 0.5cm (⅛in) seam allowance, stitching through all the layers and making sure you catch the ribbon.

3. Place the washbag in front of you, pocket side up. Fold over a 1cm (¼in) hem at the starting end of the bias binding. Then, open out the bias binding (see Figure 7). Starting in the middle of the bottom edge, place and pin it, right sides together, all around the edges. Machine stitch in place (see pages 150–51 for how to attach bias binding).

4. When you get back to where you started, trim the binding so that you have an overlap of 2cm (¾in).

5. Turn over the washbag, fold the bias binding over to the other side, then use ladder stitch (see page 149) to hand-sew in place.

6. Hand-sew one half of a popper in the centre of the top edge, about 1cm (¼in) down. Close up the washbag, allowing plenty of room for when it is full, and position and stitch the other side of the popper in place.

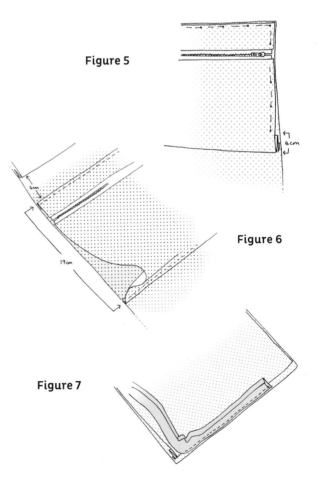

Figure 5

Figure 6

Figure 7

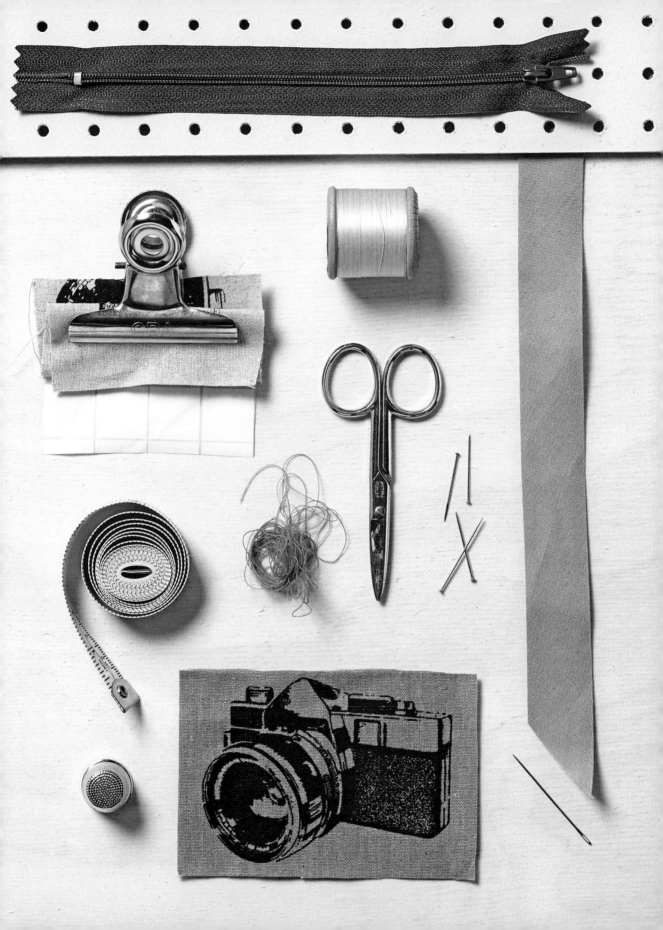

Bed linen set

TIME

YOU WILL BE ABLE TO TRANSFORM YOUR BED LINEN WITH THIS DELIGHTFUL PROJECT IN JUST AN EVENING OR TWO.

A pretty bed linen set really makes a room, but beautiful linen can be so expensive, and to make your own requires huge amounts of fabric. This version is much simpler and cheaper, and more effective. You can take a really simple plain-coloured bed linen set and add a little trim of fabric to make all the difference. The fabric I chose is my favourite Liberty print at the moment, and I think it would look beautiful in my little girl's bedroom!

MATERIALS

THESE QUANTITIES ARE FOR A SINGLE DUVET SET, BUT YOU CAN INCREASE THEM FOR ANY DUVET SIZE (SEE STEP 1, OVER THE PAGE).

LIGHTWEIGHT COTTON FABRIC (PILLOWCASE AND DUVET TRIM): 150CM X 100CM (60IN X 40IN)

BED LINEN SET (2 PILLOWCASES AND A SINGLE DUVET COVER)

CO-ORDINATING POLYESTER THREAD

TOOLS

TAPE MEASURE

FABRIC SCISSORS

PINS

IRON

SEWING MACHINE

NEEDLE

PREPARE THE FABRIC TRIM

1. To find out the size of the fabric trim you'll need for your duvet and pillowcases, measure the width of the duvet cover and add 4cm (1½in). Make a note of this, as this is the length of your duvet trim. Now take a pillowcase, measure the width and again add 4cm (1½in). Again, make a note of this, as this is the length of your pillowcase trim.

2. Cut a rectangle of trim fabric measuring 35cm (13¾in) x the duvet trim length. For the pillowcases, cut two rectangles measuring 20cm (8in) x the pillowcase length.

3. One fabric rectangle at a time, turn each edge toward the wrong side by 2cm (¾in). Pin and iron in place.

TRIM THE LINEN

1. Iron a pillowcase. Place one of the pillowcase fabric strips on top, right side up. Line up the long edge of fabric trim with the short, open end of the pillowcase; and the two short edges of fabric trim with the top and bottom of the pillowcase. Pin in place, making sure you catch only the top layer of pillowcase fabric. Sew around the edge of the fabric trim with a 0.5cm (⅛in) seam allowance, stitching the trim to the top layer of the pillowcase. You can do this by hand using running stitch (see page 148) or using your machine set to straight stitch, reversing at the start and end to secure your stitching. (See Figure 1.) Repeat for the other pillowcase.

2. Iron your duvet cover to remove any wrinkles, and lay it right side up. Lay the duvet cover fabric trim on top, also right side facing up. Line up the top edge of the duvet cover with the top, long edge of the fabric trim, and the two short edges of the fabric with the sides of the duvet cover. Pin in place, ensuring you pin through only the top layer of the duvet cover.

3. The bulk of the duvet cover can wreak havoc if you trim the duvet using your machine, so you'll probably find it easier to sew the duvet trim by hand. Hand-sew around the edge of

the fabric trim using running stitch with a 0.5cm (⅛in) seam allowance. If you do use your machine, open out the duvet cover and place the fabric panel under the machine needle. You'll have lots of bulk, so be careful. Machine stitch around the edge of the fabric trim with a 0.5cm (⅛in) seam allowance. Reverse stitch at the beginning and end to secure. It can get a little tricksy with so much fabric to manoeuvre, especially at the corners, so take your time.

TIP

To add more detail, try sewing a length of ric-rac or lace along the edge of the fabric strips, where they meet the bed linen.

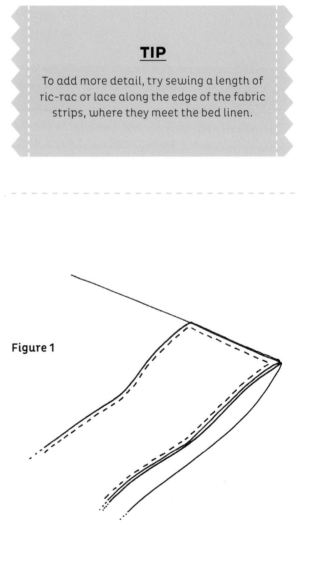

Figure 1

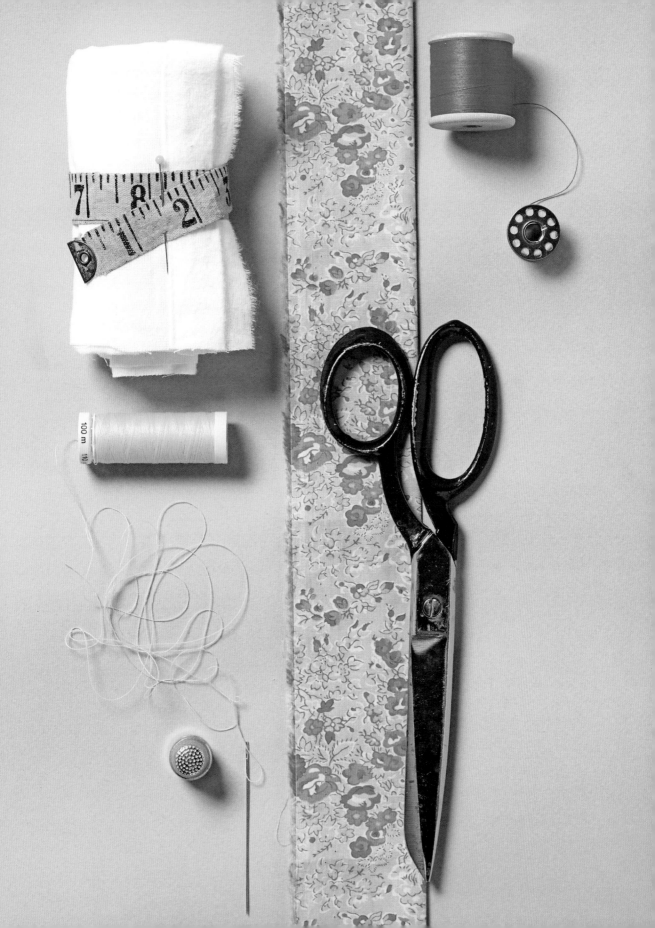

DOORStOP

TIME

SET ASIDE THREE HOURS TO COMPLETE THIS PROJECT, OR A MORNING.

We used to live in a flat in London with wooden floors and heavy doors – they would make such an enormous bang as they swung shut. We needed doorstops aplenty! None of them were quite as lovely as this one, though. You can use fabrics to tie in with a room's decor, or go for something neutral – whatever you fancy.

MATERIALS

CYLINDRICAL SIDE AND TIES PATTERNED HEAVYWEIGHT COTTON FABRIC: 75CM X 25CM (30IN X 10IN) (SEE PAGE 110 FOR CUT SIZES)

TOP AND BOTTOM PLAIN COTTON FABRIC OR LINEN: 2 X PIECES, EACH MEASURING 15CM (6IN) IN DIAMETER)

CO-ORDINATING POLYESTER THREAD

POLYESTER STUFFING: APPROXIMATELY 30G (1OZ)

RICE: 2KG (4½LB)

TOOLS

TAPE MEASURE

FABRIC SCISSORS

PINS

SEWING MACHINE

IRON

TAILOR'S CHALK OR ERASABLE FABRIC PEN (OPTIONAL)

NEEDLE

CUT OUT YOUR FABRIC PIECES

1. From your patterned fabric, cut a rectangle 42cm by 23cm (16½in x 9in) – this will be the main cylinder shape. Then you will need two smaller rectangles from the same fabric each measuring 30cm x 8cm (12in x 3¼in) for the ties. Finally, if you haven't already, cut out two circles 14cm (5½in) in diameter (a small plate or a bowl is usually about right) from the plain fabric for the top and bottom pieces.

SEW THE PARTS

1. Fold the large rectangle in half, matching up the short ends, right sides facing. Pin to hold the two short sides of the rectangle together. Now machine stitch down the edge of the short sides with a 1.5cm (½in) seam allowance. Reverse stitch at the beginning and end to ensure the stitching is strong. Iron it out flat (see Figure 1).

2. To make the two ties that form the handle, take one of the small rectangles and fold it in half, right sides facing, matching up the two long edges. Pin in place. Machine stitch across one of the short ends and down the long edge. Reverse at the start and end of your stitching. Leave the other short end open – you'll turn the fabric the right way out through this hole. Clip the corners (see page 150), then turn the tie the right side out. Iron flat. Repeat for the other small rectangle.

PUT IT ALL TOGETHER

1. Take one of the circular pieces of fabric and fold it in half. Mark the point on either side of the semi-circle where the fold occurs (use your tailor's chalk or fabric pen, or make a crease between your fingers). Open out the fabric – you will have marked the midpoints of two sides of the circle. Right side uppermost, pin the short unfinished end of one tie to one midpoint, with the raw edges lined up. Fold up the bulk of the tie and pin it to the centre of the circle, so that it is clear of the impending hem! Repeat for the other tie, on the opposite midpoint.

2. Lay the circle with ties attached out in front of you, right side up, and position your cylinder of fabric on top (see Figure 2), with one edge of your cylinder joining the circle. Lightly pushing

the edge of the cylinder flat against the circle, pin the two pieces together (see Figure 2). Sew around the circle, with a 1cm (¼in) seam allowance. (This can be a bit fiddly – take your time, repositioning your cylinder fabric around the circle as you go, if you need to.)

3. Repeat Step 2 for the other end of the doorstop, this time leaving a 7cm (2¾in) gap in the seam so that you can turn the doorstop through the right way. Clip the curves (see page 150), making sure you don't cut too close to your stitching.

4. Turn the doorstop through the right way. Pop some stuffing into the top section, giving it some padding, then pour in your rice.

5. Hand-sew the 7cm (2¾in) gap closed using ladder stitch (see page 149), then unpin the ties and tie them together in a knot on top as the handle for your doorstop.

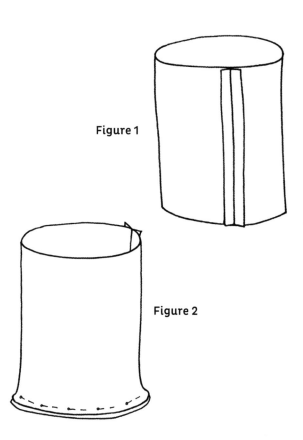

Figure 1

Figure 2

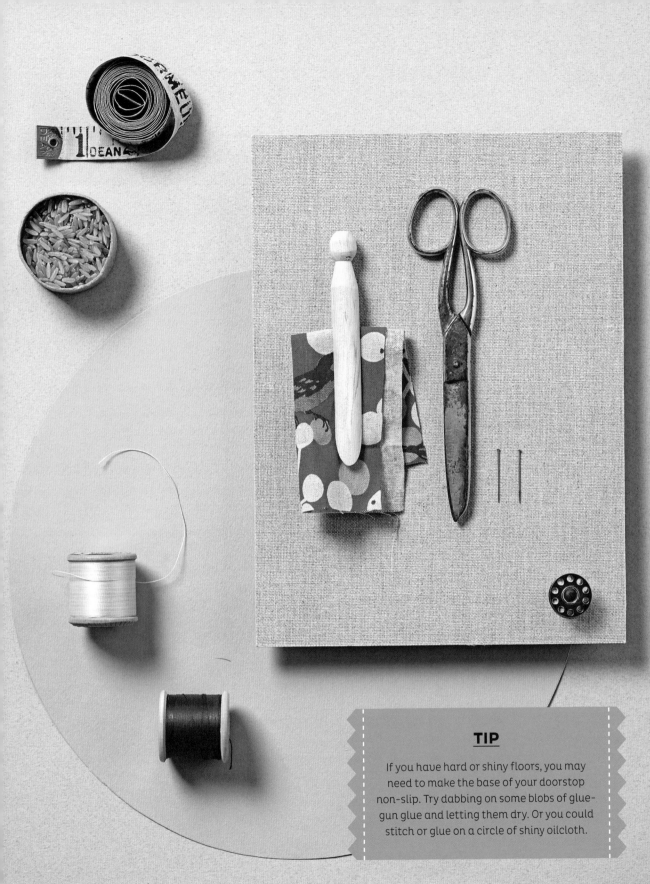

TIP

If you have hard or shiny floors, you may
need to make the base of your doorstop
non-slip. Try dabbing on some blobs of glue-
gun glue and letting them dry. Or you could
stitch or glue on a circle of shiny oilcloth.

vintage doily cushion

I'm not one for crocheted doilies on the table, but I totally appreciate their appeal, so I wanted to include them in some way. I also wanted to make a cushion for the book – I love how a cushion can really dress a room, making all the difference. So here we have it: a cushion with a crocheted doily on top.

TIME

PUT ASIDE A COUPLE OF MORNINGS OR EVENINGS – THERE ARE A FEW FIDDLY BITS IN THIS PROJECT.

TOOLS

PATTERN PIECE PROVIDED AT THE BACK OF THE BOOK

TAPE MEASURE

PINS

SEWING MACHINE

PENCIL

PAPER SCISSORS

FABRIC SCISSORS

IRON

NEEDLE

MATERIALS

CUSHION FRONT LIGHTWEIGHT COTTON FABRIC: 19CM X 110CM (7¾IN X 44IN)

CROCHETED DOILY: 10–20CM (4–8IN) DIAMETER

CO-ORDINATING POLYESTER THREAD

CUSHION BACK LIGHT- TO MEDIUM-WEIGHT COTTON OR LINEN FABRIC: 25CM X 80CM (10IN X 32IN)

ROUND CUSHION PAD: 33CM (13IN) DIAMETER

2 X POPPERS: 1CM (¼IN) DIAMETER

MAKE THE DOILY FRONT

1. Fold your piece of front fabric in half, right sides together, matching the short ends. Pin in place. With your machine set to straight stitch, sew along the short edge with a 1cm (¼in) seam allowance, to create a wide tube.

2. To gather this into a rosette shape, set your sewing machine to its longest straight stitch. Sew two lines all around the tube: the first 1cm (¼in) in from the edge and the second 1.5cm (½in) in from the edge. Leave a long tail of thread at both ends, and don't reverse stitch at the beginning and end: you need the ends to be free.

3. Grip one end of both threads in one hand, and the other end of both threads in the other hand. Carefully pull on the threads and push the fabric gently to gather it. Gradually work the gathers as tightly as they will go, pulling the fabric into a rosette. (See Figure 1.) Tie a knot in the threads and trim the ends.

4. With the right side of the cushion front facing upward, place the doily in the centre of the rosette and smooth it down lightly. Pin on the doily, trying to keep the fabric gathers as evenly spaced as you can – although this design is quite forgiving.

5. Set your sewing machine to a medium straight stitch and re-thread it if necessary with a colour that matches your doily. Sew all around the doily, about 1cm (¼in) in from the edge, to fix it to the cushion front.

SEW UP THE CUSHION

1. Trace the cushion back piece from the back of the book, then using your paper scissors, cut it out. Fold the cushion back fabric in half, pin on the pattern piece and cut out two back pieces.

2. Take one of the back fabric pieces and fold over the straight edge by 1cm (¼in) and then 3cm (1⅛in) toward the wrong side, to form a wide hem. Iron in place.

3. Re-thread your sewing machine with co-ordinating thread. Straight stitch along the inner edge of the hem, leaving a 0.5cm (⅛in) seam allowance. Repeat with the other back piece.

4. Lay the two back pieces so that the straight sides overlap by 4cm (1½in), both with right sides upward, to make a complete circle. Pin together.

5. Now lay the front fabric (with the doily), on top of this back circle, right sides facing. Pin the layers together, keeping the gathers as evenly spaced as you can. Sew all around the cover, with a 1.5cm (½in) seam allowance. Reverse stitch at the beginning and end to secure. (I find it slightly easier to do this step with the gathered fabric on top. It won't match the backing fabric precisely at the sides, so don't worry if they aren't perfectly even.) Clip the curves (see page 150) to remove some of the bulk of fabric. Remove the pins from the centre back and turn the cushion cover right side out.

6. Hand-sew the poppers on to the hem allowances of the cover opening to create a fastening.

Figure 1

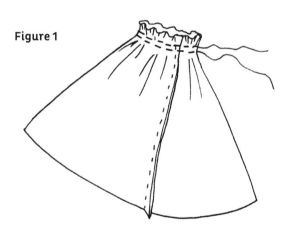

TIP

If you don't have any doilies, you can buy new ones cheaply in bed linen and tableware shops (see page 154 for stockists), or check second-hand stores.

foldaway bread platter

I love bread! And a good loaf deserves good presentation. I wanted this platter to be quite rustic. Hannah, who tested this project, found an alternative use for it – or, rather, her kitten Maple did. Instead of a bread platter, Hannah now has a well-loved kitten bed!

MATERIALS

2 X PIECES OF MEDIUM- TO HEAVYWEIGHT COTTON OR LINEN FABRIC: 50CM X 60CM (20IN X 23½IN) EACH (YOU COULD USE TEA TOWELS CUT TO SIZE, IF YOU LIKE)

HEAVYWEIGHT IRON-ON INTERFACING: 50CM X 60CM (20IN X 23½IN)

COTTON TAPE: 2CM (¾IN) WIDTH X 150CM (60IN) LENGTH

CO-ORDINATING POLYESTER THREAD

TOOLS

TAPE MEASURE

IRON

RULER

TAILOR'S CHALK OR ERASABLE FABRIC PEN

FABRIC SCISSORS

PINS

SEWING MACHINE

NEEDLE

PREPARE THE FABRIC

1. Iron the interfacing to the wrong side of one of the pieces of fabric, following the manufacturer's instructions.

2. Measure, mark and cut out a 9cm x 9cm (3¾in x 3¾in) square at each corner. Repeat with the second piece of fabric.

3. Cut the tape into eight equal-length pieces and pin each piece of tape to the centre of one of the raw edges on the right side of the interfaced fabric. Pin the trailing ends in toward the centre, so they won't accidentally get caught in a seam. (See Figure 1.)

SEW THE PLATTER

1. Place the second piece of fabric on top, right side down and matching the raw edges. Pin in place. With your machine set to straight stitch, sew round the edges with a 1cm (¼in) seam allowance, leaving a 15cm (6in) gap on one of the long edges. Make sure you don't accidentally catch any pieces of cotton tape in your stitches.

2. Clip all the corners (see page 150), then turn the platter right side out, making sure you push fully into all the corners. Iron flat.

3. Turn in the raw edges of the 15cm (6in) gap. Pin in place, then iron flat. Use ladder stitch (see page 149) to hand-sew the gap closed.

ADD THE FINISHING TOUCHES

1. To neaten each of the ends of the tape, make a double hem: turn the tape in by 0.5cm (⅛in) and then 1cm (¼in). Machine stitch the hem through all the layers. Reverse stitch at the beginning and end to secure.

2. Topstitch where you will fold up the platter (see Figure 2) through the layers. This will help the platter to sit neatly when being used.

3. Fold each of the four side pieces toward the centre and iron in place – this will ensure a neater finish and give the shape a helping hand. When you want to use the platter, simply tie up the tapes.

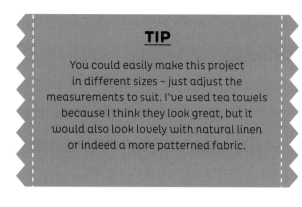

TIP

You could easily make this project in different sizes – just adjust the measurements to suit. I've used tea towels because I think they look great, but it would also look lovely with natural linen or indeed a more patterned fabric.

Figure 1

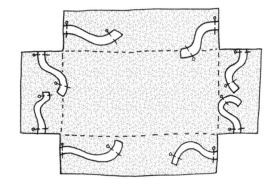

Figure 2

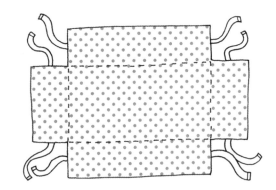

Table Place Mats

My sister has just moved house and I really wanted to make her a housewarming gift that would be both beautiful and useful. This fitted the bill perfectly, and I was able to choose fabrics that suited her colour schemes.

TOOLS

FABRIC SCISSORS

TAPE MEASURE

PINS

SEWING MACHINE

IRON

NEEDLE

MATERIALS

PRINTED LIGHTWEIGHT COTTON TRIM FABRIC: 12CM X 25CM (4¾IN X 10IN) FOR EACH PLACE MAT

PLAIN LIGHTWEIGHT COTTON FABRIC: 25CM X 28CM (10IN X 11IN) FOR EACH PLACE MAT

LIGHTWEIGHT COTTON BACKING FABRIC: 25CM X 38CM (10IN X 15IN) FOR EACH PLACE MAT

CO-ORDINATING POLYESTER THREAD

CONTRASTING POLYESTER THREAD

TRIM AND PREPARE YOUR FABRIC

1. Take your trim fabric and lay it on top of the plain fabric at the left-hand edge, with right sides together. (If you are using a patterned fabric, make sure the pattern is the right way round.) Pin in place. With your machine set to straight stitch, sew down the edge, with a 1cm (¼in) seam allowance (see Figure 1). Open out, and iron the seam toward the trim fabric.

2. Sew a line of topstitching on the patterned fabric, 2mm (⅟₁₆in) from the seam, with contrasting thread.

SEW YOUR MATS

1. Take the back piece of fabric and place it on top of the two pieces you have just joined together, right sides together. Pin in place. Machine stitch around the edge, with a 1cm (¼in) seam allowance and leaving a 10cm (4in) gap on one of the long edges.

2. Clip the corners (see page 150) and turn the mat right side out, pushing right into the corners as you do so.

3. Iron the mat flat, then turn in the raw edges of the gap and hand-sew closed using ladder stitch (see page 149).

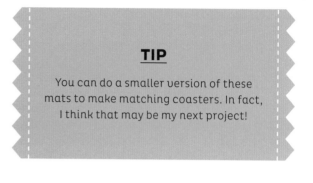

TIP

You can do a smaller version of these mats to make matching coasters. In fact, I think that may be my next project!

Figure 1

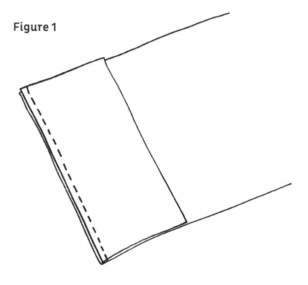

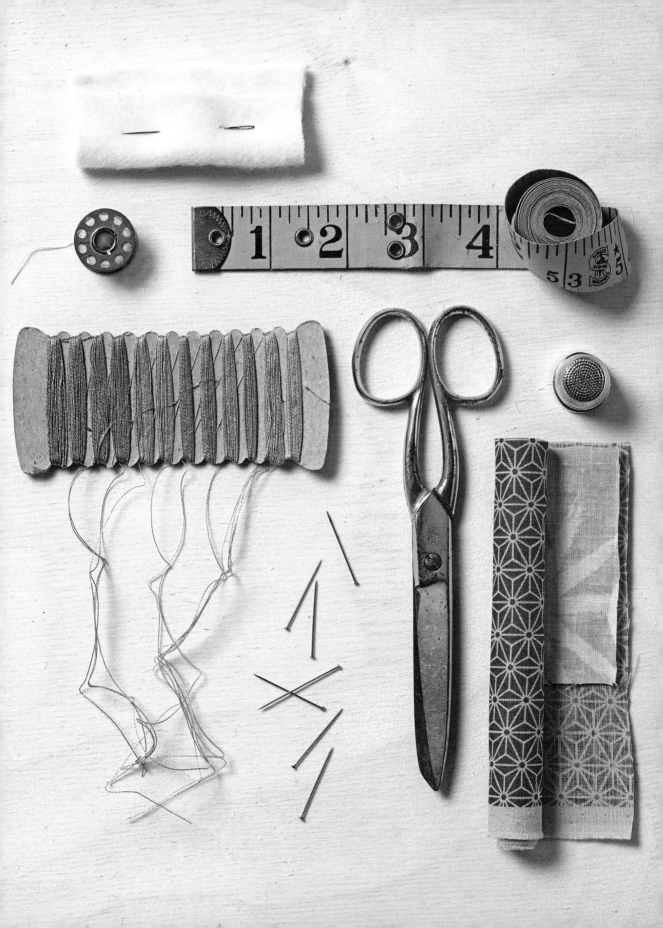

FLYING dUCKS

This is my absolute favourite project in the book. I had the idea a few years ago and made a prototype, which has been waiting patiently for the right opportunity to present itself. They just look brilliant!

TOOLS

PATTERN PIECES FROM THE BACK OF THE BOOK

PENCIL

TAPE MEASURE

FABRIC SCISSORS

PINS

SEWING MACHINE

NEEDLE

MATERIALS

BACKING HEAVYWEIGHT COTTON FABRIC: 35CM X 90CM (13¾IN X 35½IN)

FRONT LIGHTWEIGHT COTTON FABRIC: 35CM X 30CM (13¾IN X 12IN)
PER DUCK

THICK FELT: 10CM X 8CM (4IN X 3¼IN)

CO-ORDINATING POLYESTER THREAD

POLYESTER STUFFING: 50G (1¾OZ)

CUT YOUR PATTERN PIECES

1. Trace or cut out the pattern templates from the back of the book. There are four pieces for each duck, so you'll have 12 pieces in total.

2. Place the pattern pieces on the correct fabric (as indicated on the pattern pieces). Pin in place, transfer all the markings from the pattern pieces, and cut out. As there are so many pieces and this is a reasonably time-consuming project, it's wise to store all the pattern pieces pinned to the fabrics and in an envelope or plastic wallet until you need them.

SEW THE WINGS

1. Let's start with duck number 1, the largest. First sew the darts in Duck Front 1 (the front body piece). To do this, fold the fabric along the dart lines with right sides together. Pin in place. With your machine set to straight stitch, sew along the lines. (See page 150 for tips on how to sew darts.)

2. Now the wings. Take one Duck Wing 1 in the front fabric, and one in the backing fabric. Place them on top of each other, right sides facing and edges lined up. Pin together. Machine stitch around the edge with a 1cm (¼in) seam allowance. Leave the bottom straight edge open. Repeat for the other pair of Duck Wing 1 pieces.

3. Clip the curves and corners (see page 150) on both wings, and turn the wings right side out through the open edge. Stuff them lightly (you don't want them too firm). Then machine stitch the gap closed, about 0.5cm (⅛in) in from the raw edge.

MAKE THE BODY

1. Take the felt Duck Beak 1 and place it on top of the Duck Back 1 piece with right sides facing, the beak pointing toward the middle. Pin in place (see Figure 1). Take the body front piece and place it on top of the body back piece, matching up the edges and right sides facing. Pin in place. Machine stitch around the outside with a 1cm (¼in) seam allowance. Leave a gap along the top between the points shown on the pattern. (This is where you will insert the wings.)

2. Clip the curves and corners, then turn the body right side out through the gap. Carefully push all the corners out, then stuff the duck with your filling. Again, you don't want it to be really firmly stuffed as it will be too bulbous, and will make inserting the wings too difficult. I would say a light-to-medium stuffing is perfect!

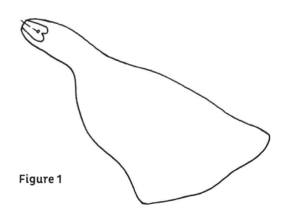

Figure 1

ATTACH THE WINGS

1. In the gap, fold the raw edges in toward the inside by 1cm (¼in) – as if to complete the seam – and pin in place. Press them with your fingers as if to iron them. Remove the pins, then take one of the wings and insert it into the gap so that the front edge is butted up to the front of the gap. Pin the wing in place, attaching it to the backing fabric.

2. Take the second wing and insert it into the gap, with the back edge butted up against the back of the gap. This should mean that the front wing is slightly further back than the back wing. Tilt this front wing down slightly at the back, so that it is on an angle (see Figure 2). Pin both wings in place through all the layers of fabric (there are a lot). You'll have to remove the first set of pins you popped in for the first wing. Take your needle and thread, and hand-sew the wings in place, while also closing the gap, using ladder stitch (see page 149) through all the layers. You'll need to pull the threads reasonably taut to close the gap and ensure everything is held in place. Secure your threads at the start and end.

3. Finally, using your needle and thread again, make a small loop on the back of the back wing. To do this, tie a knot at the end of your thread, make two or three small stitches without pulling the thread all the way through, and then secure your stitches. (See Figure 3.)

MAKE THE REMAINING DUCKS

1. Repeat the making process for the medium (pattern pieces 2) and small (pattern pieces 3) ducks. Then arrange the ducks and hang them on the wall for all to admire!

Figure 2

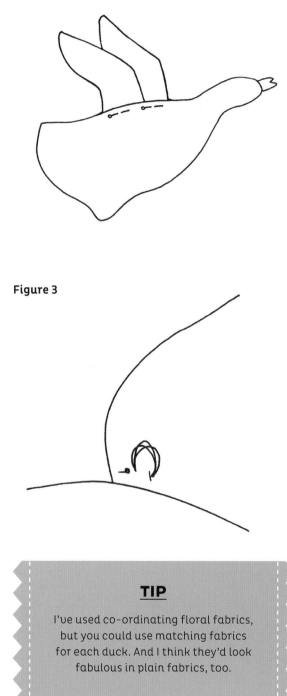

Figure 3

TIP

I've used co-ordinating floral fabrics, but you could use matching fabrics for each duck. And I think they'd look fabulous in plain fabrics, too.

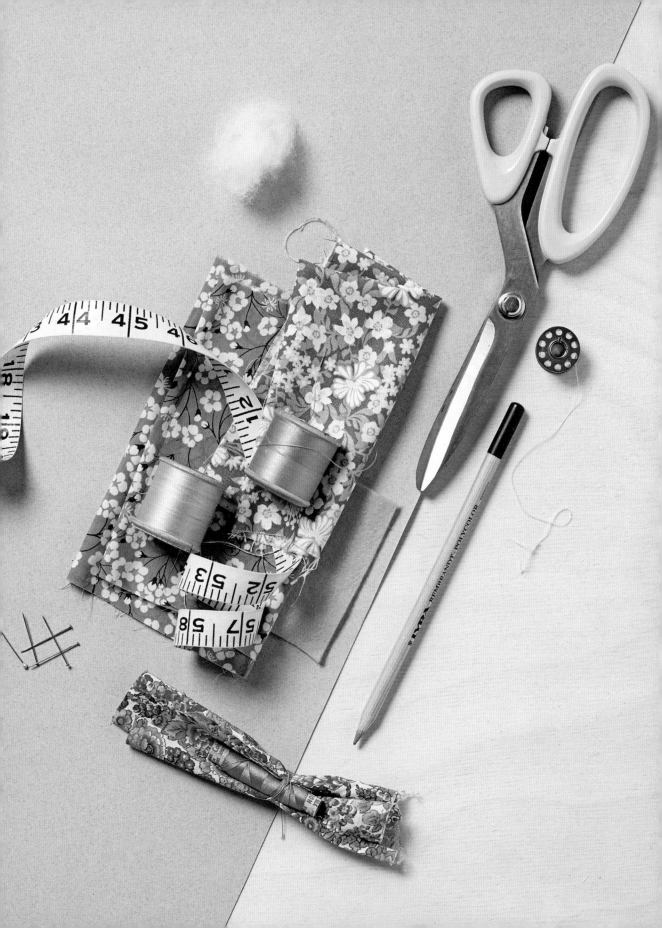

Guest towels

These are nice as a not-too-tricky gift for someone – perhaps as a last-minute housewarming gift. It's also an attractive and effective way to liven up cheaper towels and give them a premium touch, with just a bit of fabric.

MATERIALS

TOWELS

DECORATIVE FABRIC: APPROXIMATELY 12CM X 50CM (4¾IN X 20IN) PER TOWEL

CONTRASTING OR CO-ORDINATING POLYESTER THREAD

TOOLS

TAPE MEASURE

FABRIC SCISSORS

IRON

PINS

SEWING MACHINE

CREATE YOUR DECORATION

1. Measure the width of your towel and add 3cm (1⅛in). Cut out a piece of fabric measuring this width by 12cm (4¾in) deep.

2. Iron your fabric strip on the wrong side. Fold over all four raw edges by 1cm (¼in), toward the wrong side, and iron in place.

SEW ON YOUR DECORATION

1. Turn the fabric over and position it on the towel, covering the woven panel. Pin in place. If your towel doesn't have a woven panel, place the fabric around 15cm (6in) up from one short edge.

2. Machine stitch all around the edges, leaving a 0.5cm (⅛in) seam allowance (see Figure 1). Reverse stitch at the beginning and end to secure.

TIP

If these are for a gift, you could embroider or stamp the person's name or initials on the fabric before you stitch it on. And you could make a matching flannel, too.

Figure 1

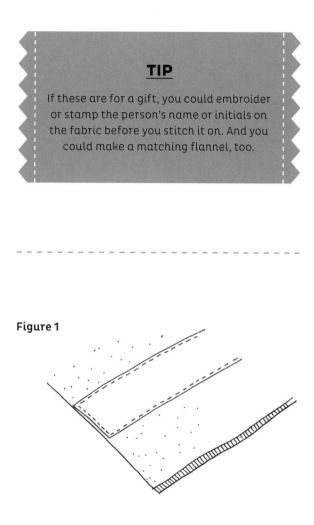

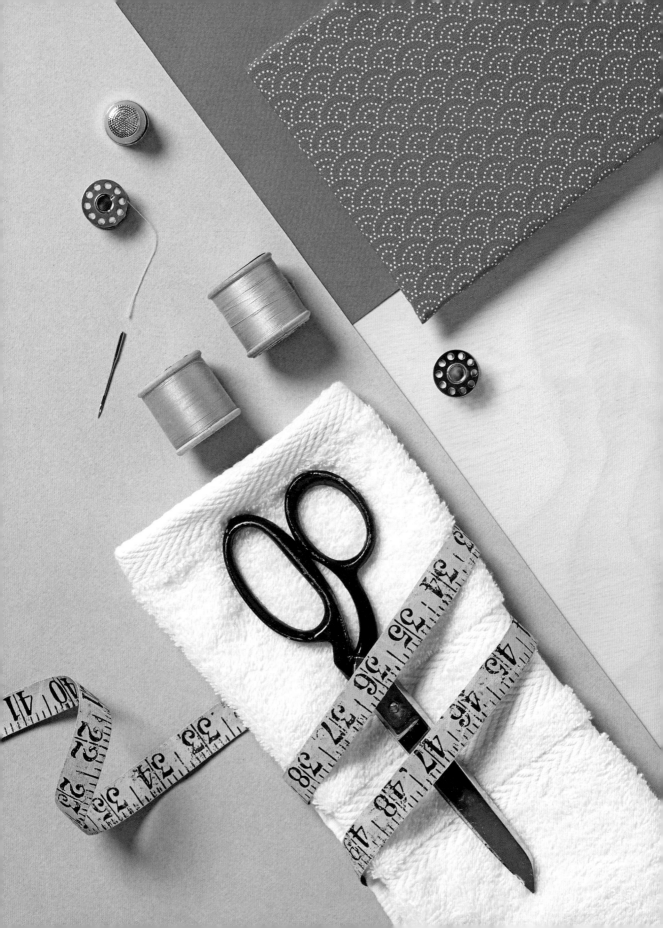

Storage box

The beauty of making your own storage boxes is that you can choose exactly the colour scheme that you want, and you can fit them to your own shelf dimensions. I've used muted fabrics, but bright ones would be ideal to bring colour into a bathroom, or make vivid storage for a playroom.

MATERIALS

HEAVYWEIGHT IRON-ON INTERFACING: 46CM X 48CM (18IN X 19IN)

OUTER HEAVYWEIGHT COTTON OR LINEN FABRIC: 46CM X 48CM (18IN X 18¾IN)

LINING HEAVYWEIGHT COTTON OR LINEN FABRIC: 46CM X 48CM (18IN X 18¾IN)

SMALL PIECE OF CALICO FABRIC: 10CM X 5CM (4IN X 2IN)

CO-ORDINATING POLYESTER THREAD

LABEL CONTRASTING LIGHTWEIGHT COTTON FABRIC OR CALICO: 5CM X 8CM (2IN X 3¼IN)

STAMPS AND FABRIC INK (OPTIONAL; WE RECOMMEND VERSACRAFT OR STAZON)

TOOLS

IRON

RULER

TAPE MEASURE

TAILOR'S CHALK OR ERASABLE FABRIC PEN

FABRIC SCISSORS

PINS

SEWING MACHINE

PREPARE THE FABRIC PIECES

1. Lay the interfacing onto the wrong side of the outer fabric, shiny (glued) side down. Iron the interfacing onto the fabric following the manufacturer's instructions.

2. In each corner of the outer fabric, mark a square 13cm x 13cm (5in x 5in), using the ruler and the tailor's chalk or fabric pen, and cut out. Cut squares out of the lining fabric corners in the same way.

ATTACH THE CALICO LABEL

1. Position the calico piece on the right side of the outer fabric – it will be on the front of your box. Pin in place. Set your machine to straight stitch and sew in place, stitching 0.5cm (⅛in) in from the edge. Go twice round to secure – don't worry if the two lines of sewing don't quite match, that's all part of the charm. (See Figure 1.)

SEW THE BOX

1. Take the outer fabric and fold in each of the side flaps toward the centre, wrong sides facing. Iron in place (the creases make sure your finished box sits neatly). Repeat with the lining, but this time with the right sides facing.

2. On the outer fabric, right sides facing, draw together the two cut edges of the square at one corner, to start forming a box shape. Using straight stitch again, machine stitch these edges together with a 1cm (¼in) seam allowance. (See Figure 2.) Repeat on the other three corners of the outer fabric, and all four corners of the lining. Press open all the corner seams.

3. Turn the outer fabric box right side out and place the lining fabric box inside the outer, matching up the four corners and edges carefully. Turn the raw edges in toward each other by 1cm (¼in). Pin in place, iron and then topstitch all the way around, leaving a 0.5cm (⅛in) seam allowance. (Take care to catch all the layers as you go.)

4. Iron the corners of the fabric cube if necessary, so that the box sits squarely on a flat surface. Once you are done, you can personalize the box by stamping a message, label or name on to the calico, if you wish.

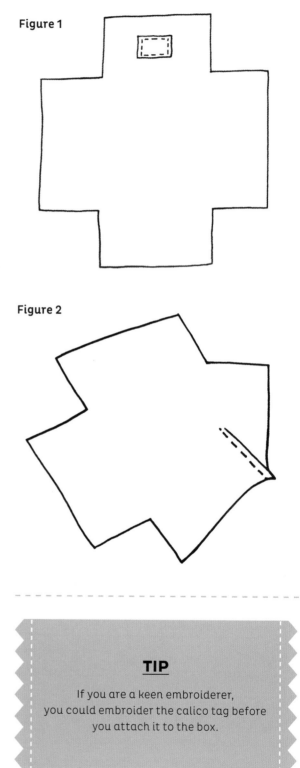

Figure 1

Figure 2

TIP

If you are a keen embroiderer, you could embroider the calico tag before you attach it to the box.

Padded oven mitt

This is a surprisingly satisfying project. It's one of those items that comes together in the final stages. You could choose fabric to match someone's kitchen – that would make a thoughtful gift, indeed.

MATERIALS

PATTERN PIECES PROVIDED AT THE BACK OF THE BOOK

LINING MEDIUM-WEIGHT COTTON OR LINEN FABRIC: 50CM X 60CM (20IN X 23½IN)

OUTER MEDIUM-WEIGHT COTTON OR LINEN FABRIC: 50CM X 60CM (20IN X 23½IN)

HEAT-RESISTANT WADDING (SEE PAGE 154 FOR STOCKISTS): 50CM X 60CM (20IN X 23½IN)

BIAS BINDING: 2.5CM (1IN) WIDTH X 60CM (23½IN) LENGTH

CO-ORDINATING POLYESTER THREAD

TOOLS

PAPER

PENCIL

PAPER SCISSORS

PINS

FABRIC SCISSORS

TAPE MEASURE

IRON

TAILOR'S CHALK OR ERASABLE FABRIC PEN

SEWING MACHINE

NEEDLE

PREPARE YOUR MITT PIECES

1. Trace the oven mitt top, bottom and grip pattern pieces onto paper and cut out using your paper scissors. Pin the three pattern pieces on your lining, wadding and outer fabrics and cut each out in turn, making sure you mark points A and B with tailor's chalk or erasable fabric pen. You will end up with the top, underside and grip in outer, lining and wadding (nine pieces in total). Iron the fabric pieces flat.

2. Take the three oven mitt top pieces and stack them together: the lining (right side down), then the wadding, then the outer (right side up). Pin the pieces together. With your sewing machine set to a long straight stitch, sew the pieces together with a 0.5cm (⅛in) seam allowance. Sew all the way around the outside, making sure you catch all the layers. This stitching is simply to hold everything together nicely.

3. Repeat the same process for the bottom and grip. You should be left with three padded pieces in total.

SEW THE MITT TOGETHER

1. Place the oven mitt grip on top of the mitt top with the outer fabrics facing. Line up the curved edges and match points A and B. Pin together, then re-set your machine to medium straight stitch and sew from A to B, with a 1cm (¼in) seam allowance. Reverse stitch at the beginning and end to secure. (See Figure 1.)

2. Fold the free edge of the grip upward, back on itself. Place the oven mitt bottom on top of this, with the outer fabrics facing. Match the curves and points A and B as before. Pin and machine stitch as above. (See Figure 2.) Clip all the curves (see page 150).

3. Now pin together the straight side edges from A down to the open end, and from B down to the open end. Machine stitch these two seams with a 1cm (¼in) seam allowance, reversing at the beginning and end to secure. Make sure you leave the bottom edge open! Turn the mitt right side out.

ADD THE FINISHING TOUCHES

1. Open out the bias binding and, right sides facing, place the end on one of the seams (this is where your hook will be). Pin it all the way around the open end (raw edge) of the mitt. Machine stitch in place, in the first fold of the bias binding, leaving the trailing end (see Figure 3). (See page 151 for more details on how to use bias binding.)

2. Close the bias binding and fold it all the way over to the inside of the mitt, so that it covers all the raw edges. Pin in place. Hand-sew using ladder stitch (see page 149) to secure, all the way round the open end.

3. You should still have a trail of bias binding at one of the side seams. Fold this in half to close it, then turn in a 0.5cm (⅛in) hem at the end to neaten. (If the bias is too long, trim it a little.) Machine stitch down the length of the trailing piece to hem it closed. Make a loop with the bias binding and machine stitch in place near the seam to form a hanging loop. Stitch backward and forward several times so that it is secure.

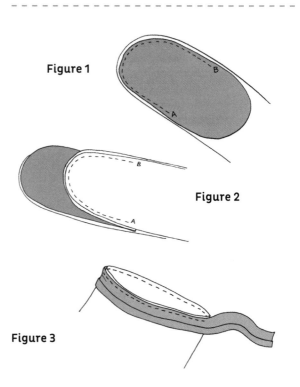

Figure 1

Figure 2

Figure 3

TIP

To make sure that your oven mitt is completely safe for holding hot pans, it is worth seeking out proper heat-resistant wadding. For stockists see page 154.

sweet-tin foot stool

TIME

GIVE YOURSELF A WEEKEND, AS THIS IS A MEATY PROJECT. OR TACKLE IT IN SEVERAL STAGES.

At my gran's house my sisters and I used to sit on these little foot stools, all in a row. She had made them specially, from brown-gold velvet, and I always thought she had used sweet tins for the base. But my mum told me recently that in fact it was golden syrup tins, taped together. So this project is for my gran, Nina — I'm sure she'd love to see my modern take on her creation.

MATERIALS

LARGE SWEET (OR BISCUIT) TIN

HEAVYWEIGHT COTTON FABRIC: 50CM X 110CM (20IN X 44IN)

PIPING CORD: 100CM (40IN)

WADDING: 50CM X 110CM (20IN X 44IN)

BIAS BINDING: 2.5CM (1IN) WIDTH X 100CM (40IN) LENGTH

POLYESTER STUFFING: APPROXIMATELY 50G (2OZ)

CO-ORDINATING POLYESTER THREAD

TOOLS

LARGE SHEET OF PAPER

PENCIL

RULER

PAPER SCISSORS

TAPE MEASURE

TAILOR'S CHALK OR ERASABLE FABRIC PEN

FABRIC SCISSORS

IRON

PINS

SEWING MACHINE (WITH ZIPPER FOOT)

NEEDLE

CUT EVERYTHING OUT

1. First make the bottom pattern piece. Lay a large sheet of paper (a sheet of newspaper would do) out flat and place your sweet tin on top. Draw accurately around the tin and cut out. This is the bottom pattern piece.

2. Place this pattern piece on the remaining paper and draw around it, this time leaving a 1cm (¼in) margin all round, making the top pattern piece 1cm (¼in) bigger than the bottom piece. Cut out the top pattern piece.

3. Measure around the side of the tin to find its circumference. Note the measurement. Measure the height of the tin and note that down, too.

4. Using a ruler and tailor's chalk or a fabric pen, mark a rectangle along one edge of your fabric that is the circumference measurement plus 5cm (2in) by the height plus 5cm (2in). Cut out this side strip.

5. Now lay the bottom pattern piece and top pattern piece on the remaining fabric. If you have an interesting print (as on my version), position the top pattern piece carefully to frame a nice image. Pin in place and cut out both pieces.

6. Using tailor's chalk or the fabric pen, mark a rectangle on your wadding that measures the exact height by the exact circumference of the tin. Cut out the wadding side strip. Fold the remaining wadding in half and pin the bottom pattern piece onto it. Cut out around the pattern to give two wadding pieces.

MAKE AND FIX THE COVERED PIPING

1. Cut a piece of piping cord to the length of the circumference of the tin plus 6cm (2⅓in). Cut a piece of bias binding to the same length.

2. Open the bias binding out flat. Place the piping cord in the centre on the wrong side, and fold the bias binding in half over it. Pin together to hold the cord firmly in between, down the full length of the cord and bias binding.

3. Attach the zipper foot to your sewing machine. Straight stitch down the length of the bias tape, close to the piping cord.

4. Lay the top fabric piece right side up and pin the bias-covered piping all around it, matching all the raw edges together. Leave a trailing end of piping (of equal length) at the start and finish. Mark the point where the two parts of the bias-covered piping meet with a pin (see Figure 1).

5. With the zipper foot still attached, sew all the way around the edge on the flat bias binding, close to the piping cord, to attach the piping to the top fabric. Begin sewing 3cm (1⅛in) in from the marker pin. Continue all the way around, keeping close to the piping, and finish 3cm (1⅛in) before you get back to the pin. (See Figure 1.)

6. Trim the ends of the piping cord so that they meet and butt up against each other at the marker pin. Trim the bias binding to leave an extra 1cm (¼in) beyond the piping at each end.

7. Open out the ends of bias binding and overlay them under the piping. Turn the outer piece of bias binding in by 0.5cm (⅛in), to neaten the edge.

8. Stitch the gap closed, overlapping with the existing stitching and reversing at the beginning and end to secure.

Figure 1

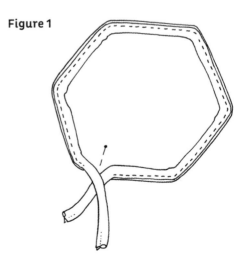

COVER YOUR FOOT STOOL

1. Lay the piped foot-stool top right side up. Take the long side strip of fabric and, with right sides together, pin it around the edge of the top, matching up the raw edges. The bias-covered piping will be sandwiched in between.

2. Using the zipper foot, stitch all the layers together, close to the piping. Leave the first 2cm (¾in) of the side strip free, and stop stitching when you reach the point where you began. Reverse at the beginning and end of the seam to secure. Trim the strip of fabric to leave 2cm (¾in) at both ends. This is your fabric cover.

3. Stretch the long piece of side wadding around the side edge of the tin. It should be taut (trim it if it's gaping at all). Hand-sew together the two ends of the side wadding. Place one wadding piece on the top of the tin and sew the side piece to the top all the way round the edge. Turn the tin over, place the other wadding piece on the base of the tin and sew this tightly in place, too, stretching it taut as you go. (See Figure 2.)

4. Put the stuffing on to the wadding top, spreading it out roughly – don't worry if it looks like a lot, as it will be compacted.

5. Take the fabric cover, turn it right side out and pull it down over your padded tin, catching the stuffing inside. Use ladder stitch (see page 149) to hand-sew the two side edges together, pulling tight (it's really important you get a tight fit).

CREATE A PROFESSIONAL FINISH

1. Turn the tin upside down. Working your way around the tin, pull the raw edges of the outer fabric up over the bottom and pin in place on the wadding base. Go round several times, pulling and re-pinning more fabric each time, until you have stretched the fabric as taut as it will go. (Just think how much use this foot stool will get – you don't want the fabric to go baggy.) When you're happy with the stretch, hand-sew the fabric to the wadding base with a few large stitches, just to last you until the next step. (See Figure 3.)

2. Take the bottom fabric piece, turn over a 1cm (¼in) hem to the wrong side of the fabric all the way around and iron in place. Place the bottom fabric piece on the base of the tin to hide all the raw edges. This will leave a 1cm (¼in) gap all the way around the edge. Hand-sew to the stretched sides of fabric using ladder stitch.

Figure 2

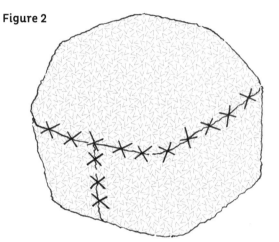

Figure 3

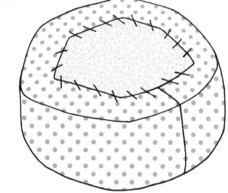

TIP

Instead of plain bias binding, you could make your own from the same or a contrasting fabric (see pages 150–51).

Stitches & tips

If you are new to sewing, here are some basics to get you going and to help you give your projects a really professional-looking finish.

HAND-SEWING

HOW TO START WITH AN INVISIBLE KNOT

1. Fold your thread in half to make a double thread, and pass the two cut ends through the needle. (The other end will be a loop.)

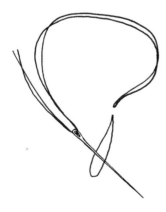

2. Starting on the right side of the fabric, push the needle through and then bring it back up again a tiny distance from where it went in, being careful not to pull the thread all the way through. You should have a loop of thread, through which you can push your needle. Pull the thread taut, and it will be secured without a bulky knot.

STITCH GUIDE

RUNNING STITCH

This can be used as a decorative stitch – it's nice and simple. Or it can be used to tack, or hand-sew pieces together that won't undergo too much stress. You can use double thread for more strength, if you like.

1. Thread a needle and knot the end. Bring the needle up through the back of the fabric.

2. Push the needle in and out of the fabric at regular intervals, following the line that you would like to stitch. You can vary the length of the stitches, and I don't push the needle in and out more than about three times at once, to ensure a nice even stitch.

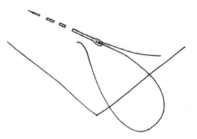

3. Pull the needle through and repeat.

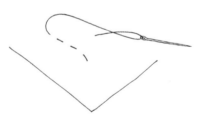

BACK STITCH

This is stronger than running stitch, so used for seams and hems when you need more strength in the stitching. You can also use it as a decorative stitch.

1. Thread a needle and knot the end. Bring the needle up through the fabric.

2. Take one stitch through the fabric, then bring the needle up one full stitch length further along your stitching line.

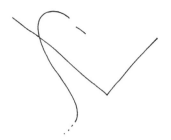

3. Put the needle into the point where your first stitch ended.

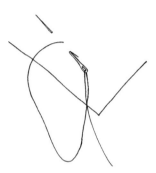

4. Bring the needle out a stitch length ahead of the previous finished stitch.

5. Keep working in this way to create a continuous line of stitching.

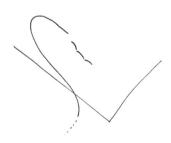

LADDER STITCH

This is one of my favourite stitches and I use it to join two pieces of fabric together.

1. Thread a needle and knot the end. Bring the needle up through the fabric on one side, where you'd like your stitching to begin.

2. At the same point on the other side of the gap to be closed, push the needle in and then out again, in the direction of stitching.

3. Keep working your way along the fabric, from one side to the other.

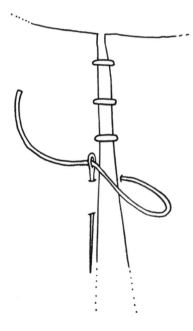

4. Pull your stitching taut every few stitches. The stitches will be almost invisible, and nice and strong.

TIPS FOR SUCCESSFUL SEWING

PREPARING FABRIC

It is sensible to pre-wash all fabric before you start any sewing project. This is to avoid shrinkage after you've made your item. Iron all pieces, too.

IRONING AS YOU SEW

Usually I'm not very friendly with my iron. However, ironing your seams as you go can make the difference between a project that looks okay, and a project that looks really professional.

PINS

I always use glass-headed pins for sewing – mainly because, unlike plastic-headed pins, they don't melt under the iron. They also look pretty and are easier to spot than metal-headed pins if you drop them.

Some people swear by pinning perpendicular to their stitching and sewing over the pins, but I am an advocate of pinning in the same direction as the line of stitching and removing the pins as you go. It's important that the pinheads are facing you, to make removing them easier.

TACKING

Tacking fabric in place with hand stitches means you don't need to manoeuvre your sewing machine around pins. You can use cheap tacking thread in a colour that stands out against your fabric and make reasonably large stitches (around 2cm/¾in long). Simply remove the tacking stitches once you've machined over them.

If I'm honest, I rarely tack these days. However, if you're making something that is either extremely important, that uses very fine fabrics, or that has lots of fiddly corners, it is wise to tack.

CLIPPING CORNERS

This removes bulky fabric to make your finished piece look far neater. I like to use a sharp pair of embroidery scissors, as they're small. When you've sewn the corner, with the fabric still inside out, snip off the tip of the corner diagonally, making sure you leave at least 3mm (⅛in) between your cut and the line of stitching. Then turn the fabric right side out and iron flat.

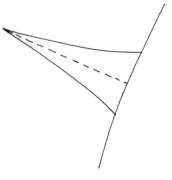

CLIPPING CURVES

This removes bulk, giving a smoother curve. When you've sewn the curve, make small V-shaped snips around it – I use small embroidery scissors – leaving at least 3mm (⅛in) between the tip of your cut and the line of stitching. Turn the fabric right side out and iron flat.

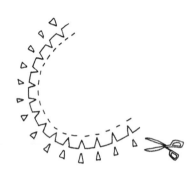

DARTS

Darts add shape and dimension to a flat piece of fabric. You make them by stitching triangles and removing wedges of fabric. There are various types of dart, but I'll show you how to make a single dart as used in the Flying Ducks project (see pages 124–9). This is what the dart markings look like on your pattern. This slightly curved dart gives a softer finish (more often, dart lines are completely straight).

1. Transfer the markings to your fabric using tailor's chalk.

2. Fold the fabric, right sides together, along the central dotted line – so that the solid lines match up – and pin along the solid lines as shown. (Pin according to the direction shown, and add a pin across the dart at the point – I do this so that I know where I'm heading as I stitch.)

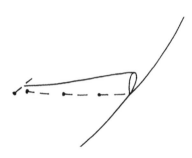

3. With your machine set to straight stitch, begin sewing at the widest end of the dart – reverse a little to secure the stitching. Carefully sew along the pinned line. When you reach the pointed end, don't reverse. Instead, leave the threads long so that you can tie them in a knot and avoid a bulge on the right side.

MAKING BIAS BINDING

Bias binding is an excellent way to trim your items to give them a professional finish. You don't need as much fabric as you might think. The following method makes more than 5m (16ft) of bias binding from just one fat quarter of fabric (50cm x 55cm/20in x 21½in). It's a bit fiddly, but bear with it – it's fab!

1. Fold your fabric at right angles. Cut along the fold line, to make two triangles. One of the triangles will have an extra strip along the edge – cut that edge off, so that you have two equal-sized triangles.

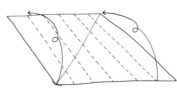

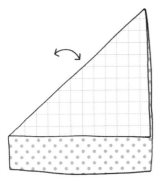

2. Flip one of the triangles and place them one on top of the other, right sides facing.

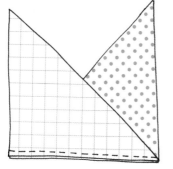

3. Pin and machine stitch along the straight edge where the triangles are lined up with a 1cm (¼in) seam allowance. Iron the seam open.

4. With tailor's chalk, mark lines that are 5cm (2in) apart all the way along the diagonal (bias) on your fabric.

5. Now the fiddly bit: fold the fabric in half, but slightly on the skew. Match up the drawn lines, but the end of the first line needs to match up with the beginning of the second line. (See the arrows shown above.) Pin along this edge where the lines meet up, and machine stitch with a 1cm (¼in) seam allowance. Iron the seam open.

6. Cut along your chalk lines to give a continuous strip of bias.

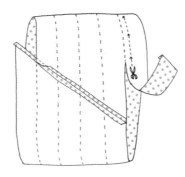

7. Fold the fabric into bias tape. Using a bias-maker (a wonderful invention!), put the end of the strip into the bias maker, and then iron it into shape. If you don't have a bias maker, fold the strip in half lengthways, and then fold the two long edges in toward the centre.

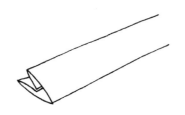

SEWING WITH BIAS BINDING: CORNERS

To bind and cover the raw edges of a piece of sewing, bias binding is a wonder! It's easier to use cotton bias, as it tends not to slip as much. And if you're a newbie, use the wider stuff.

1. Open out the bias binding and match up the right edge to the raw edges of your fabric. Pin in place, and machine stitch in the ditch of the first fold in the bias binding.

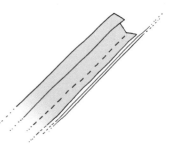

2. Slow down as your first corner approaches. Stop 1cm (¼in) before you get to the end, put the needle down and raise the presser foot. Pivot your fabric so that you're pointing in the direction of the corner of the fabric. Lower the presser foot and finish the line of stitching to the corner point.

3. Cut your thread, and remove the fabric from the machine.

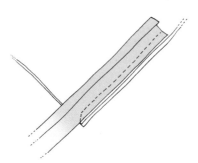

4. Fold the bias binding down so that the edge follows the raw edge of the fabric, and pin in place.

5. Starting a new line of stitching at the top edge, machine stitch in the ditch of the fold of the bias again, as you did along the previous edge. Repeat for all corners.

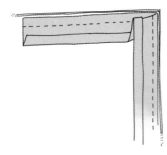

SEWING WITH ZIPS

Zips can be quite off-putting, but don't worry – use your zipper foot attachment on your sewing machine, as this has notches either side, where your needle goes. The notches mean that you can sew close to the teeth of a zip, but the metal of the foot itself means that you shouldn't sew over the zip.

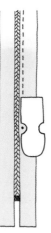

Always start to sew a zip with the zip half open, then stop stitching a few centimetres (an inch) before you reach the zipper pull. Put your needle down into the fabric and raise the presser foot. Move the zipper pull backward, toward the beginning of your sewing. When your zipper pull is a few centimetres clear of the presser foot, lower the presser foot again and continue stitching to the end. This way, you won't have to negotiate your way around the zipper pull and risk a wobbly line.

HAND-SEWING A BUTTONHOLE

Mark the position of the buttonhole with tailor's chalk or a fabric pen. Cut along the line where the buttonhole will open. With a needle and buttonhole thread (which is much stronger), stitch two lines of running stitch parallel to and 3mm (⅛in) away from each side of the slit.

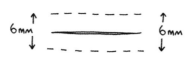

With a new piece of thread, sew a line of buttonhole stitch (see diagram, below) along the top and then bottom of the slit, working from left to right.

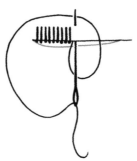

At each end sew three long stitches from top to bottom, then a small row of stitches that encase these.

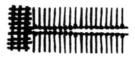

USING SEWING PATTERNS

GRAIN

Woven fabrics are made up of threads that run horizontally and vertically. The direction that the threads run is called the 'grain' of the fabric. If you try to stretch the fabric in the direction that the threads run, you'll notice there isn't really any give. On many patterns, you will see a line with an arrow at either end. It's important that this line follows the direction of the grain – to ensure the fabric sits straight on your finished piece. For example, if you were to make a skirt and the grain wasn't aligned, you'd find the skirt just wouldn't sit correctly, and would keep twisting round. Not a good look!

BIAS

The bias of a woven fabric runs diagonal to the grain. If you try to stretch the fabric on the bias, you'll notice it has quite a lot of give in it. Fabric cut on the bias hangs in a much softer way, owing to the stretch. Note that this doesn't apply to knitted (jersey) fabrics.

SELVEDGE

The finished edge of a whole width of woven fabric, the selvedge often has a white unprinted strip. It's useful for checking the grain of the fabric.

NOTCHES

You'll notice little triangles at the edges of some pattern pieces. Where you see them, it's important that you cut the notches into your fabric – they are there to ensure you match pattern pieces accurately.

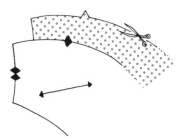

SEAM ALLOWANCE

This is the distance between your stitching and the edge of the fabric. The plate below your sewing machine's presser foot should have markings that will help you measure the seam allowance as you sew.

USING A SEWING MACHINE

STARTING AND FINISHING YOUR STITCHING

You always need to secure your stitching to ensure it doesn't come undone. The quickest and sturdiest way of doing this is to make a few reverse stitches.

AT THE START

1. I think it's good practice to do the very first stitch of any line manually. That way, you have complete control over where your stitching begins and the speed at which you're sewing. Turn the balance wheel toward you until the needle has completed one stitch. (Turning the wheel away can knot the threads.)

2. Lower your foot on the pedal and sew three or four stitches. Then hold down the reverse lever (check your manual for its whereabouts) and make three or four stitches backward, sewing over your previous stitching. Now you're good to keep sewing.

AT THE END

1. When you've finished your stitching, hold the reverse lever down and make three or four stitches back over your work.

2. Raise the presser foot and pull out your fabric, trimming the thread close to your stitches.

WITH FINE FABRICS

1. Rather than reversing, leave a long tail at the start of your stitching. Turn your fabric wrong side facing upward.

2. Hold the thread at the end of the stitching and give it a pull to bring a loop of thread.

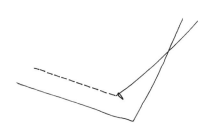

3. Pull this loop with a pin.

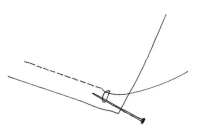

4. This will pull the upper thread through to the back. Then knot the two threads together securely.

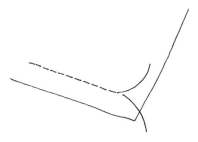

SEWING MACHINE MAINTENANCE

NEEDLE

If your machine starts missing the odd stitch, your needle could be blunt and need changing.

OIL

Many machines come with a little bottle of oil. If not, sewing machine retailers will sell one. It's worth oiling your machine monthly if you use it regularly.

If it starts to sound less happy and doesn't run as smoothly as it should, brush all the collected dust from the bobbin area and give it a good oil. Make sure you do a piece of test sewing afterwards, in case some of the oil transfers to your fabric.

stockists

Crocheted doilies
www.shawsthedrapers.co.uk
www.etsy.com

Embroidery hoops
www.themakery.co.uk
www.purlsoho.com

Fabric pens
www.themakery.co.uk
www.joann.com

Gütermann HT2 glue
www.themakery.co.uk
www.americanpursesupplies.co

Heat-resistant wadding
www.barnyarns.co.uk
www.themakery.co.uk
www.joann.com

Interfacing
www.themakery.co.uk
www.joann.com

Iron-on vinyl
www.themakery.co.uk
www.joann.com

Pendant bases
www.themakery.co.uk

Purses clasps
www.themakery.co.uk
www.americanpursesupplies.co
www.u-handbag.com

Ribbon
www.themakery.co.uk
www.purlsoho.com

**Solvy water-soluble
fabric stabilizer**
www.barnyarns.co.uk
www.joann.com

**Split-ring keyrings, D-rings,
side-fastening clasps**
www.themakery.co.uk
www.americanpursesupplies.co
www.u-handbag.com

**Stamps and Versacraft and
Stazon stamping inks**
www.themakery.co.uk
www.simonsaysstamp.com

Twine
www.themakery.co.uk
www.purlsoho.com

INDEX

><<<<<<<<<<<<<<<<<<<<<<

NOTES, INSPIRATION & MEASUREMENTS

Acknowledgements

Thank you to Denise Bates and all at Octopus Publishing Group for your support in making this book possible.

Marc Wilson, Martha Gavin, Aliki Kirmitsi, Ania Wawrzkowicz and Maya Wilson, and Luke Wright and Ross Imms at A-Side Studio: you've made the pages so wonderfully flickable and brought the projects to life beautifully, thank you.

An extra-big thank you to Judy Barratt for keeping on my back in such a friendly way to make sure I got everything done on time (sort of). And for your excellent editing skills.

All the lovelies who tested the projects; young and old, new and seasoned sewers: Emma Abel, Martha Barratt, Jan Biagioli, Ella Davison, Silvana Dean, Claire Feltham, Caroline Harris, Betty Hebditch, Audrey Horne, Yeli Horswill, Vicky Millar, Zola Purdie, Mark Sabine (check out his blog talesfrommothersruin.wordpress.com), Sue Smith, Eliza Solesbury, Hannah Surman, Pauline Vaughn and Elena Woods. All your feedback was invaluable.

Our photography would not have been possible without our locations: thank you to Lynn Swain of the wonderful 4 Beaufort boutique b&b in Bath (www.4beaufort.co.uk), Felicity Lynch for use of her beautifully stylish flat (www.felicitylynch.co.uk) and the Porter, for use of its lounge and café (www.theporter.co.uk). We are also grateful to Sam's Kitchen (www.samskitchendeli.co.uk), Made By Ben (www.madebyben.com), the Julian House shop in Walcot Street and the Holburne Museum, Bath. A really big thank you to Emma Wynne, for her help with the photoshoots.

Thank you to gorgeous Sarah Cunniffe, Cerys Gasson and Lucy Dacey for your most brilliant sewing skills in making the pyjama shorts, doorstop, laundry bag and tie projects for me.

Thank you to Jess Butler for looking so pretty and modelling some of the spreads for us! Thank you to Emily Langdon for your help with the writing. And to all our wonderful staff at The Makery for helping us with our dream: Sarah, Cerys, Alice, Jess, Katie, Allie, Lyndsey, Caroline, and all our freelancers – we're lucky to have you involved. A special mention for Alice Bradley who never fails to impress me, and manages to hold things together while we're haring all over the place. Thank you!

Caroline Harris and Clive Wilson – thank you for making it a reality in the first place, and bringing everything together.

And finally, of course, thank you to Nigel. You're my hero! I'm so lucky we found each other for our life's adventure.